Weight Loss
Cookbook

MODA Nutrition Inc.
81 Navy Wharf Court
Suite 3212
Toronto, ON M5V 3S2
Canada

ISBN-13: 978-1979411752
ISBN-10: 1979411751

Printed in the United States

Cover design: Karen Piovaty Designs
Interior design: Jordi Hayman and Rachel Little
Cover photos: Nicholas Li and Tony Vassallo
Roasted Fennel Vegetables (page 77): Grant Ruston
All other photos: Tony Vassallo

Weight Loss
Never Tasted
So Good
COOKBOOK

*To Luke and Mike – two friends that left us way too early,
and to my grandmother, Nana – thank you for all the memories.*

Contents

Meet Tony!

Greetings! I'm Tony Vassallo, founder of MODA Nutrition Inc. and Man on a Nutrition Mission™. Since an early age it has been a dream of mine to write a cookbook. I never would have imagined it would be a healthy-living cookbook based on my decades of unhealthy living. Now I embrace my new lifestyle and passionately preach it. My story starts in 2010: I was thirty-seven years old, weighed over three hundred pounds and was classified as morbidly obese. I detested the reflection I saw in the mirror to the point that I removed all full-length mirrors from my home. I cringed when I was referred to as a "big guy."

Though I gained "just a few pounds" every year, I started to fear for my future. I had a host of medical issues: diabetes, hypertension, sleep apnea, gout, joint pain, constant indigestion and acid reflux. Simple tasks like putting on socks, climbing a flight of stairs, fitting into an airplane seat or booth at a restaurant and getting out of bed became big challenges for me. Every afternoon I would have a sugar crash, leaving me with little energy to get through the rest of the day. I was always sweaty and tired. I began avoiding the outdoors and eventually just avoiding life.

Reality began to set in when my 48-inch pants started to get snug and it was time to put on the 50-inch pair. I looked at pants and said, "My God, these are like drapes." I had many wakeup calls while I continued to exponentially gain weight but this one hit me like no other. I finally admitted I was not only fat but morbidly obese, the biggest classification of fatness. I couldn't use words like "husky," "chunky," or "big-boned" anymore – I was morbidly obese.

At one point it became apparent I might never live to see life beyond my 40s. I sought to change all that once and for all. Over the next year, I lost a hundred and thirty pounds and have maintained a cool one-seventy pounds ever since. I have been on mission to help others do the same – eat and think their way to a healthy weight in a safe, sustainable way with real food.

Ironically, what I thought would be my biggest liability in losing weight – my love of good food – turned out to be my strongest asset. I was able to take my passion for creating culinary masterpieces and adapt them to add a nutritional twist. Using my culinary training, many thousands of hours of Food Network viewing, my constant yearning for dietary information and my expansive cookbook collection, I discovered how to create healthy, satisfying meals that did not leave me feeling deprived. I transformed myself from an eat-everything-in-sight foodie to a healthy foodie.

Then and Now Stats:

Then

- BMI: 40.1 (morbidly obese)
- Heaviest recorded weight: 304 pounds
- Waist: 50 inches
- Neck: 19.5 inches
- Metabolic Syndrome

Now

- BMI: 23.0 (normal)
- Current weight: 170 pounds
- Waist: 32 inches
- Neck: 15.5 inches
- Medication-free for over five years and counting

The Early Days

"The definition of insanity is doing the same thing over and over again and expecting different results." — attributed to Albert Einstein

Going from Former Fat Guy to Man on a Nutrition Mission™ was no easy feat (in the beginning). But I had to change. I couldn't continue to keep eating and living the way I was. Being fat, sick, frustrated and tired left me fearing for my future. I had to be more open-minded about living a healthy lifestyle but it was hard. I wanted nothing to do with rabbit food. I got offended if I was offered a salad. I didn't want to be the same room as healthy food. The first several weeks of eliminating refined foods gave me serious withdrawal. I found going for constant mini-walks for five or ten minutes helped. I would go for a quick five-minute walk around my building as soon as I got up, then another ten minutes at lunch and squeeze in ten to fifteen minutes after dinner. While I'm sure the exercise was beneficial, its main benefit was a chance to be by myself and remind myself of the importance of changing my life before it was too late. I also carved out a few hours on Saturday morning or Sunday afternoon to take a long walk in a park. This gave me a chance to plan out the week in my head and to be one with nature. I discovered many hidden treasures in Toronto such as High Park, Toronto Island, areas along the southern Ontario waterfront and many other parks in my area that I had never seen before.

My taste buds started to change and I began to enjoy the natural flavor of fruits and veggies. Whole grains became palatable, lean protein that was not soaked in fatty sauces was enjoyable. I later learned that our bodies actually crave the nutrients in these foods, not the processed foods. We need to reset our taste buds and cleanse them of that garbage. I refer to this as going back to our primitive, "default" taste buds.

The Project

"In order to succeed, we must first believe that we can." — Nikos Kazantzakis

Once I got over the initial weight loss hump, I could sense a shift in myself. I had so much more energy and that empowered me to continue. I began to believe that I could and would do this. I was able to find creative and tasty ways to make healthy food enjoyable. Unknowingly, I made a project out of it when I started taking pictures of most of my meals. At first it was to remind me of dishes I created so I could refer to them later. Soon I had an entire library of meal pictures. I will share many of them with you in this book.

Advice for the Initial Days

- Take this journey one day at a time
- Focus on quality of food and not so much on quantity at first
- Set your first long-term weight loss goal for 5% of your body weight
- Eliminate confectionary items, snack foods like potato chips, nachos, etc. – having a little will only taunt and tease you to have more
- Don't fret over slipups or bad days. Success is not a straight line

My Mantras

- Eat real food: Have a lean protein and a complex carbohydrate source at every meal
- Eat fewer packaged items
- Eat lots of veggies – and I mean LOTS
- Reach for fruit when you need something sweet
- Drink lots of water
- Prepare and plan your meals in advance
- Have three meals and three snacks a day; no cheating!
- Don't skip meals!
- When buying pre-made food, choose items with five ingredients or fewer… the fewer the better
- Your home must be in the zone: Remove all junk food in your home
- Set realistic goals and follow through
- There are no solutions inside the refrigerator

The Transition, The Metamorphosis

As you lose weight you will feel a massive shift inside you, mentally and physically. You will become stronger and what at first seemed impossible becomes very possible. You will begin to envision a happier, healthier you. That success will create a domino effect of many more successes. You will find it easier to push back the pie, turn down the dumplings and resist the ribs. You will want to take a walk instead of watching TV. You will begin to wear clothes that haven't fit in years. You will sleep better, you will think clearer and you will feel more energetic than you ever have before. You will hear compliments, and you may even be the subject of some envy. Strangers will make eye contact, smile and say good morning. You will embrace a mirror as opposed to shunning it. You will start to make love with the lights on… everything is possible.

Weight loss is not achievable via a fad diet, starvation, or whatever the latest gimmick is. The common denominator of all successful long-term weight loss stories is that the people behind them made a permanent lifestyle change. All the recipes and tips I share with you in this book will help you make that lifestyle change. The most important piece of advice I can give you is that in order to maintain your weight loss, you must maintain the same healthy habits that helped you lose your weight and carry them into your maintenance phase.

"Passionate. Knowledgeable. Caring. These are the three words that best describe Tony Vassallo. Tony's commitment is why I am here today – his support through my personal transformation allowed me to achieve my health goals and his advice and personal touch [are] ensuring that I continue on the path that I set out on. I owe Tony my deepest gratitude – and my life." — Drew

"I've known Tony for several years now and have always enjoyed his genuine passion for all things nutrition and lifestyle. He's got a very real world approach and is constantly coming up with new ideas, researching better ways and means. Tony traveled the road of weight loss, has truly been 'there' and is doing the right things now moving forward. He is a sharing individual who believes in collaboration and I find his approach very entertaining and easy to follow, understand and execute." — John

"Tony Vassallo has developed an easy way of sharing his vast knowledge of nutrition. I found Tony when I was sixty pounds overweight and overwhelmed by the volume of conflicting Internet data about 'good' and 'bad' foods. Tony quickly connected the dots and gave me a simple way to eat everyday foods and gradually lose weight while never feeling hungry. I'm down fifty pounds in nine months and now understand why I had gained and how to keep it off by simply eating the right foods, at the right times, in the right proportions and combinations. I recommend Tony without hesitation." — Robert

"Losing weight is one thing. Maintaining is entirely another. Tony's recipes and tips have made healthier eating both delicious and fun for the whole family." — Michael and Jo'Ann

"Tony helped me lose my 95 pounds and now helps me maintain it with recipes that are simple, easy to prepare, and incredibly tasty. That's the MODA way!" — Farley

"Tony's food and recipes are fun, easy, visually appealing and incredibly tasty. I thought losing weight and eating healthy would be impossible for me; however, Tony has made it super easy and enjoyable. I have never eaten so well and looked so good. Thanks Tony!" — Tarik

"Tony's cookbook is the "Simple Plan" to a better and healthier, slimmer you… This man not only MODA-vates you but also corrects and makes you wise to food marketing ploys that helped make me a healthier and slimmer shopper." — Mauro

"Being two-thirds of the man I once was is thanks to JERF – 'just eating real food.' Learning how to make that 100% delicious and satisfying is thanks to my friend Tony and his wonderful recipes. Tony makes eating well easy and desirable!" — Scott

"Tony's recipes are exciting and delicious. He inspired me to be more creative and try things never before on my radar. I have never had anyone turn down one of my creations or Tony's either. Read it and eat! A healthy lifestyle is the only way to go. Thank you Tony." — Fred, maintaining a 47-pound weight loss for three years

Introduction

The Mission

Even as I was losing weight myself, I was already encouraging other people in their weight loss journeys. I realized I had a gift and I had found my true calling in life. After almost 20 years of working in various call centers and on the hardware side of technology, it became apparent to me that culinary nutrition was where my true passion lied. Once I reached my goal weight, I went back to school to study Nutrition and Wellness at George Brown College. In my spare time, I researched anything and everything I could on weight loss, nutrition and food addiction. I began following authors and wellness experts such as Michael Moss, Michael Pollan, Marion Nestle, Dr. Robert Lusting, Dr. Vera Tarman, Dr. Colin Campbell, Dr. Neal Bernard and many more.

I began healthy culinary workshops, spending all my free time researching topics related to nutrition, weight loss and addiction. I spent over three years at a men's weight loss program as a keynote speaker providing educating and coaching to hundreds of men.

Then in 2015, I created MODA Nutrition Inc., based in Toronto, so I could continue my mission to help others lose weight and improve their health.

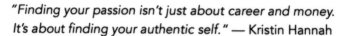

"Finding your passion isn't just about career and money. It's about finding your authentic self." — Kristin Hannah

A Guide to Getting Started

"Don't eat anything a third grader cannot pronounce." — Michael Pollan, *Food Rules*

Have three meals and three snacks a day: Each meal should consist of a lean protein source and complex carbohydrate source.

Focus on quality: If there is one thing I wish to instill in you in terms of your foods choices, it is be sure to eat real, quality food. Real food is food you can visualize or understand what it is: that is, food that looks like food. As Jamie Oliver says, "Real food does not have ingredients, real food is the ingredients."

Review nutritional labels and ingredient list to understand the degree of processing. Below are a few guidelines.

- One-ingredient items are best, the fewer ingredients the better
- Make sure you can recognize and understand all the ingredients in an item
- Choose only 100% whole wheat/whole grain breads and bread alternatives (whole wheat crackers); avoid white bread
- Choose whole grain/bran cereals or cooked cereals with little or no added sugar; add fruit instead
- True whole grain products will have a carbohydrate to fiber ratio of 10:1 or better
- Choose unrefined grains and starches such as brown, red, black or wild rice, whole wheat pasta, spelt, kamut, quinoa, barley, bulgur, etc. Avoid white rice and/or white pasta

Be aware of and avoid added sugars. When purchasing prepared foods, sauces, yogurts, breads and cereals, choose brands with no added or minimally added sugars. Review the ingredient list to determine the sugar content. Avoid or dilute 100% fruit juices with water.

Eat lots of vegetables. Prepare veggies with minimal healthy oils or none at all and select a variety of fruits and vegetables. Avoid serving with store-bought sauces.

Choose lean proteins: white meat poultry, seafood, eggs, certain dairy or plant-based proteins. For beef or pork, select leaner cuts such as loin or round. Prepare your proteins in a healthy way: broil, bake, grill, roast or poach.

Drink lots of water. This means 2.5 liters per day for males and 1.5 liters per day for females. Also keep in mind that the larger a person is the more water they will require.

The FDA recommends keeping your daily sodium intake around 1500–2400 mg per day. Substitute herbs and spices in place of salt.

Accurately record your food and drink intake every day using a food journal or app. You can download the MODA Nutrition Daily Food Journal at www.modanutrition.com

Introduction

Use a food scale so you can measure all proteins and carbohydrates servings. Scales can be purchased at most retail outlets such as Walmart, Canadian Tire, The Bay or other specialty kitchen stores.

No cheating! When it comes to confectionary items, potato chips, candies, or any other junk food, the slogan "Bet you can't eat just one" is correct. This might sound impossible; however as you cleanse yourself of these items you will soon find the cravings too will subside. Many people find abstinence easier than moderation.

Eat regularly and *don't skip meals.* Do not starve yourself. Always manage your hunger by having snacks between meals. You will find grazing on vegetables will help curb hunger and serve as a vehicle for transitioning from habitual unhealthy snacking.

Experiment and vary your recipes so you do not suffer from the boredom blues. I encourage you to seek out new recipes and customize them to your taste preferences so you stay on track and do not get bored. You will find tons of healthy, tasty recipes to get you started in the pages to follow.

Select a time each week to prep and plan meals. Meal planning is key to your success. Making this a habit will save you time and money. Review the pantry list on page 158 for items to stock in your pantry, refrigerator and freezer.

"Failing to plan is planning to fail." — Alan Lakein

When dining outside the home, always familiarize yourself with restaurant meals or options by visiting their websites or calling and asking in advance. This is true for all functions whether they be business or social occasions. Ask servers or the chef how meals are prepared and be comfortable asking for changes or substitutions if necessary. Most establishments are more than happy to accommodate your request(s) and if they are not, you can choose to go elsewhere. These rules also apply when traveling for vacation or business.

Remove any junk food from your home so you are not tempted. This is crucial for any items you cannot resist. Alcoholics do not keep alcohol in their homes. Food addicts are no different. Very few people can have just one of their favorite snacks. One leads to a few; a few leads to many; before you know it, you are binge-eating. Many times a heart-to-heart conversation with those around you can achieve a resolution. My experience from the hundreds of people I have coached over the years is that healthy living becomes contagious. Many parents want to lead by example.

Inform family members, friends, close colleagues and anyone else in your life of your commitment to healthy living. Keeping this to yourself will be of no benefit and you will need the support of everyone around you, especially in the beginning. If you find resistance (intentional or unintentional) you need to question the relationship or see them less often or avoid eating situations with them.

Inform your physician and monitor any medication(s).

Find a weight loss support group. For those in the Greater Toronto Area, you can visit www.modanutrition.com to find out details of current Man on a Nutrition Mission™ Workshop Information or look into local support groups in your area.

"There are many examples of the power of a group in supporting you to change your behavior. [They] encourage and create enthusiasm, accountability, and a degree of energy that keeps you motivated. Just being on a shared journey can create a sense of connectedness that can keep you motivated, engaged and enthusiastic."— Omar Manejwala, *Craving: Why We Can't Seem to Get Enough*

Triggers

As you progress in this journey you will become more aware of your triggers for certain foods ("kryptonites," as I refer to them). They could be feelings, events, locations, television programs, smells, thoughts, even people or a combination of items. My advice is avoid or significantly limit exposure to these triggers and approach with caution.

Get off the couch and start moving! It does not need to be any mind-blowing regimen. Start with simple walking for 10 to 15 minutes. As you lose weight, you will be motivated to increase the time and duration of your activities. Always consult a physician regarding any issues relating to your specific conditions.

Remind yourself constantly why you decided to take on this journey. A motive is what induces a person to act, keeping you focused on your goals. Set goals. I encourage you to have short- and long-term goals. For those struggling with the concept of your ideal weight or perhaps you have a lot of weight to lose, make your first long-term goal to reach 10% of your body weight. For many, the first 10% is the hump period. Once you get over that hump, you are empowered from the success and momentum to take you to your healthy weight.

As you achieve goals and milestones, treat yourself to something as a reward for your accomplishments. Buy new clothes (being sure to eliminate old ones), a healthy cookbook or new sporting equipment. Attend a healthy cooking class. Treat yourself to a day at the spa. Take in a play or show, date night with your partner or revisit memories of your youth such as visiting your old neighborhood or high school. Take a trip. Do whatever inspires you to strive for further success.

As for food treats, think exotic fruits for snacks or desserts, or replace unhealthy proteins with high-quality fish. Replace potato chips with plain popcorn. Treat yourself with exotic vegetables, creatively prepared.

Remember, success is not a straight line. Understand that you will likely have bad days and mishaps along the way. Make every effort to avoid them, but when they happen accept them and move on. Do not dwell on any mishap.

"Fall seven times, stand up eight." — Chinese Proverb

Introduction

The Food

All the recipes in this book are the Real Meal. This is the food I ate while losing my weight. Many of them have a photo as I plated them myself. Note that the recipes have a minimal amount of salt, added sugar and oils. Depending on your taste buds and where you are on this journey, you may want to adjust them slightly. For many of us, our threshold tolerance for salt and sugar is way too high and we need to bring them down. As your taste buds begin to adjust you will find you need much less salt in your food. I encourage you to keep any added sugars to a minimum and this too will adjust in time. Punch up recipes with herbs, spices, pure extracts (vanilla or almond), fresh black pepper, reduced stock, low-sodium hot sauces or other ethnic sauces.

Bountiful Breakfasts

Breakfast has been said to be the most important meal of the day. You know what... they're right! Why? Keep in mind that the body has been in fasting mode while a person sleeps. It's now time to break that fast, hence the name: breakfast. Many of us don't realize that what we eat in the morning sets the tone for the rest of the day, similar to the first tee of a golf game. And no, coffee and toast or a muffin is not a real breakfast, nor are almost any cold cereals. I went nearly my whole adult life never eating breakfast; now it's the meal I cherish most. As you can see in this section, I take the time to have a sit down and enjoy a cooked breakfast, making the extra effort to make it taste and look great. It is my form of morning meditation.

Protein Ideas for Breakfast

2 hard- or softboiled eggs (MODA Tip: Prepare eggs in advance)
½ cup cottage cheese, 2%
¾ cup unflavored Greek yogurt, 2–5%
¼ cup cottage cheese + 3 tablespoons hemp hearts (hemp hearts and hemp seeds are the same)

> **Tony's Tip!**
>
> Always think P + C. Have a lean protein source and a grain (complex) carbohydrate for breakfast. A cooked grain such as oats is best.

Carbohydrate Ideas for Breakfast

1–2 packets plain, unflavored instant oatmeal
2–2½ ounces rolled oats, raw
2–2½ ounces wheat cereals
2–2½ ounces bran or fiber cereal (choose cereals with no sugar)
2–2½ ounces steel-cut oats, raw
2–2½ ounces tasty and nutritious whole grain cooked cereals such as Red River or Bob's Red Mill

Ways to Add Flavor to Cooked Cereals

Fruit:
*   Fresh or frozen berries such as blueberries, blackberries, raspberries, etc. (Purchase fresh berries when in season and freeze)
*   Mashed banana
*   Grated apple
*   Unsweetened coconut
*   Dried fruit – select with no added sugars. They tend to be available at health food stores, specialty bulk stores or markets
*   Pure vanilla extract (be sure the label says "Pure")

Sweet Spices:
*   Cinnamon
*   Ground nutmeg
*   Ground cloves
*   Ground cardamom
*   Pumpkin spice blend

> **Tony's Tip!**
>
> Cooked cereals such as steel-cut or rolled oats were the carbohydrate of choice for me for breakfast more often than not. They gave me the energy I needed for the day and it wasn't until I began studying nutrition that I realized the many health benefits of oats.

Steel-Cut Oats with Fruit

Serves 1
Ingredients:
2–2½ ounces steel-cut oats
¾–1 cup milk or fortified dairy beverage, such as soy or almond milk
1 teaspoon cinnamon
1 apple, grated with peel (or other fruit of choice)
Pinch of sea salt

Directions:
Place oats and milk in saucepan over medium heat. Stir constantly for 4–6 minutes.
Add cinnamon and salt.
Stir until desired consistency. Add more milk if too thick.
Serve in bowl. Top with grated apple or other fruit. Serve with protein of choice (see opposite page for ideas).

Tony's Tip!

Always keep the peel. That's where the insoluble fiber is.

Cherry Compote

Ingredients:
2 cups fresh cherries, pit removed or use frozen fruit mix
Juice and rind of one orange
1 teaspoon ground cardamom (optional)

Directions:
Combine all ingredients in small to medium saucepan over medium heat. Stir until cherries begin to liquefy, 4–6 minutes.

Tony's Tip!

Make a large batch of fruit compote and store in mason jars; they will keep up to a month or more if refrigerated. It goes great with yogurt or on top of cooked cereals!

Quick & Simple Cereal

Tony's Tip!

When choosing cold cereals, select ones with less than 5 grams of sugar and avoid ones with artificial sweeteners as they may induce cravings later in the day. As you get further into the journey, move into cooked cereals.

MODA Granola

Makes about 4–5 cups
Ingredients:
4 cups rolled oats (not quick oats) or use a blend of grains such as spelt and kamut
2–3 teaspoons cinnamon
1–2 teaspoons ground cloves (optional)
1–2 teaspoons fresh nutmeg (optional)
1–2 teaspoons fresh cardamom
½ teaspoon salt
½ cup unsweetened coconut
½ cup dried cranberries or raisins
1 cup unsalted chopped nut blend, such as walnuts, almonds, pecans or brazil nuts
½ cup pumpkin or sunflower seeds

Directions:
Preheat oven to 350°F.
Combine oats and spices including salt.
Evenly spread mixture on deep baking dish for 20–35 minutes, stirring occasionally until brown but not burned.
Remove from oven, add coconut, dried fruit, nuts and seeds.
Allow to cool on wire rack.
Store in sealed container such as mason jar.

Refrigerate or freeze. A small handful of these make for a quick snack with some fresh fruit or mixed in with yogurt and baked fruit.

Bountiful Breakfasts

Oat & Blueberry Nutty Granola Parfait

Makes 1 parfait
Ingredients:
1½–2½ ounces rolled oats
½ cup unflavored Greek yogurt, 2%
½ cup blueberries
6 almonds or 4 walnut halves
Dried cranberries or raisins for garnish

Directions:
Place three-quarters of the oats at the bottom of a tall, wide glass.
Layer yogurt, blueberries and remaining oats.
Top with nuts and dried fruit.

Tony's Tip!

Always select plain or raw nuts with no added salt.

Creamy Oat Granola

Serves 1
Ingredients:
1½–2 ounces whole oats
1 teaspoon wheat germ (optional)
¾ cup unflavored Greek yogurt, 2%
¼ cup raisins or other dried fruit such as apricots, cranberries or goji berries
1 tablespoon unsweetened coconut flakes
6 pecan halves
Dried cranberries or raisins, for garnish

Directions:
Combine oats and wheat germ (if using) with yogurt.
Add dried fruit and coconut flakes.
Top with nuts and dried fruit.

Apple & Cinnamon Power Oats

Serves 2
Ingredients:
2 medium apples
Juice of 1–2 lemons
4½ ounces rolled oats
2 tablespoons dry fruit such as raisins or dried cranberries
1–1½ cups milk, soy or almond milk
1–2 teaspoons cinnamon
1 tablespoon flax (optional)
1 teaspoon wheat germ or wheat bran (optional)

Tony's Tip!

For added fiber, add 1–2 tablespoons of wheat germ or wheat bran. Bran and wheat germ are a great way to add fiber. They make up the most nutritious part of the wheat kernel. This is the stuff most manufactures remove to increase shelf life.

Directions:
Grate apples. Soak in lemon juice to prevent browning.
Combine oats, raisins and milk in a small saucepan over medium heat. You may also substitute water.
Cook and stir for 3–4 minutes or until oats become soft.
Add grated apple with some of the lemon juice, cinnamon and optional items.
Add additional milk, if required.
Serve with protein of choice.

Berry & Cinnamon Oats

Serves 1
Ingredients:
2 ounces rolled oats
½–¾ cup milk, soy or almond milk
½ cup fresh berries
1–2 tablespoons dried cranberries or raisins
1 tablespoon flax (optional)
1 teaspoon cinnamon
1 teaspoon wheat germ or wheat bran (optional)

Directions:
Combine all ingredients in a microwave-safe bowl.
Microwave on medium high heat for 2 minutes.
Stir, cook for additional 30–45 seconds on high until oats are soft.
Add additional dairy to thin oatmeal to desired consistency.
Top with grated apple.

Pumpkin & Berry Oats

Serves 1
Ingredients:
2 ounces whole or rolled oats
1 teaspoon pumpkin spice blend
½ cup frozen or fresh berries
¾ cup milk
1 teaspoon teff, for garnish

Directions:
Combine dry ingredients in small to medium saucepan.
Add fruit and milk.
Cook over medium high heat for 5–7 minutes, stirring frequently, until oats become soft.
Serve in a bowl, garnish with teff.
Substitue teff flakes for oats for a burst of exotic earthiness. Compound with cooked sweet potatoes or pumpkin purée.

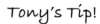

Tony's Tip!

Purchase grain flakes such as kamut or spelt flakes. They can be purchased at bulk food stores. Teff is a tiny dark-brown grain that cooks just like rice. Keep some in your fridge to add flavor to cooked cereals.

Peanut Butter Power Smoothie

Serves 1
Ingredients:
2–3 ice cubes
1 medium banana
½ cup rolled oats
2 tablespoons all-natural peanut butter
1 tablespoon ground flax or ground chia seed
¾ cup milk or fortified dairy beverage, such as soy or almond milk

Tony's Tip!

Add oats, flax or chia seeds to help create some "bulk" to smoothies; it aids in satiation.

Directions:
Combine all ingredients in a blender. Pulse until all ingredients are smooth. Pour in a chilled glass and enjoy! Serve with one slice of whole wheat bread.

Open-Face Eggs on English Muffin

Serves 1
Ingredients:
2 medium or large eggs
2 small whole grain English muffins, such as Ezekiel English Muffins
Selection of vegetables, such as sliced tomato, cucumbers or lettuce
Sprouts (optional)

Directions:
Toast English muffins.
Poach eggs using stovetop egg poacher or poach in rolling boiling water for 2 minutes. If you prefer, fry egg in a minimal amount of oil.
Assemble egg on English muffin.
Add vegetables as according to picture.

Whole Wheat French Toast

Serves 2
Ingredients:
4 medium or large eggs
¼ cup milk
Pinch of salt
4 slices whole wheat whole grain bread (preferably 2 days or older)
Dusting of cinnamon
1 tablespoon butter or cooking spray
Fresh berries or sliced banana for garnish (optional)
Nuts of choice
Cherry Compote (page 19, optional)

Directions:
Preheat griddle or skillet.
Break eggs into a large wide bowl. Lightly beat eggs with a fork.
Add milk and salt.
One at a time, place the bread slices into the bowl to soak up egg mixture for a few seconds. Turn to coat other side. Repeat with other slices.
Sprinkle each slice of bread with cinnamon on both sides.
Over medium low heat, melt butter and spread evenly on griddle or skillet or spray with cooking spray.
Transfer bread slices to griddle or skillet and cook until golden-brown on both sides, turning once.
Top with nuts, berries or compote.

> **Tony's Tip!**
>
> Older bread works best so it can soak up more of the liquid.

Super Veggie Omelet

Serves 2
Ingredients:
4 medium or large eggs
1 tablespoon olive or canola oil
½–1 cup chopped clean mushrooms
1 small onion, finely diced
½ cup red or green pepper, diced
1 cup baby spinach
Alfalfa sprouts, hot peppers, salsa for topping (optional)

Directions:
Beat eggs in a medium bowl.
Heat olive oil on medium heat in medium sauté pan.
Turn heat to medium high. Add mushrooms and sauté until they become brown.
Lower heat to medium, add onions and cook until onions are soft, 2–3 minutes. Add peppers and spinach.
Toss in pan until spinach becomes wilted.
Pour the egg mixture into the pan. Stir for 10–15 seconds to blend egg mixture with cooked vegetables.
Lift edge of egg mixture with spatula or fork until bottom of omelet is cooked and you are able to flip it.
Flip and cook for one minute then fold and serve with toast.
Top with alfalfa sprouts, hot peppers or salsa, if desired.

Tony's Tip!

Loaded with vegetables, omelets were one of my favorite meals at home breakfast or lunch. Eggs make for perfect healthy protein choice. Always choose free-range eggs. They cost more but they are worth it.

Never soak mushrooms in water. Simply brush with paper towel and trim ends.

Bountiful Breakfasts

Baked Egg & Veg

Serves 2
Ingredients:
1 tablespoon olive oil or cooking spray
1 cup sliced mushrooms, cleaned and trimmed
1 medium onion, finely minced
1 clove garlic, finely minced
2 cups fresh spinach or kale
4 medium or large eggs
Black pepper to taste

Directions:
Preheat oven to 375°F.
Heat oil in large sauté pan or wok over medium heat.
Add mushrooms. Let sit, without stirring, about 4–6 minutes or until mushrooms have caramelized.
Add onions and stir. Cook for 2–3 minutes then add garlic.
Add spinach or kale. Cook until greens become wilted.
Spray oven-safe ramekins with cooking spray.
Evenly divide vegetable mixture into ramekins.
Crack one egg into each ramekin.
Place ramekins in a baking dish that is half-filled with water and put in preheated oven.
Cook for 8–12 minutes until egg whites are cooked and yolks are desired texture.
Serve with whole wheat whole grain toast.

> **Tony's Tip!**
>
> If you wish to avoid baking, poach eggs separately and place poached eggs over cooked vegetable mixture.

Easy Microwave Eggs

Serves 1
Ingredients:
1 medium or large egg
1 small shallot, finely diced (optional)
Herbs such as oregano (optional)

Directions:
Beat egg in a microwave-safe mug.
Add shallot and herbs (if using) and place into microwave. Cook on medium heat for 60–120 seconds (microwave settings may vary).
Allow to sit for 45–60 seconds to cool.

Elegant Poached Eggs

Serves 1
Ingredients:
8–10 asparagus spears, clean and trimmed
1 tablespoon white vinegar
2 medium or large eggs
1 slice whole wheat or whole rye bread, toasted
Black pepper
Tabasco sauce (optional)

Directions:
Fill medium or large pot with water and cover. Bring water to a boil.
Blanch asparagus in boiling water for 2–3 minutes). Remove asparagus from water. Pat dry with paper towels.
Add vinegar to boiling water (This will help keep the eggs together).
Crack eggs into water and cook for 3–5 minutes. Remove eggs using a slotted spoon and place on paper towel to dry.
Assemble asparagus and eggs on toast as in photo. Bon appetit!

> Tony's Tip!
>
> Add grilled onions or mushrooms for additional flavor and nutrients.

English Breakfast

Serves 1
Ingredients:
2 thinly sliced pieces of peameal bacon, rind and fat removed
2 slices whole wheat whole grain bread or 1 whole grain bun
1 tablespoon mustard
Sliced tomato
Sliced onion or cucumber (optional)

Directions:
Grill bacon 1–2 minutes per side until fully cooked.
Assemble sandwich with bacon and remaining ingredients.

Quinoa Breakfast Bowl

Serves 1
Ingredients:
½ cup quinoa flakes
1 cup milk or fortified dairy beverage, such as soy or almond milk
½ teaspoon pure vanilla extract (optional)
Fresh fruit of choice

Directions:
Combine quinoa flakes milk, and vanilla in small saucepan over medium heat. Cook, stirring, for 4–6 minutes.
Stir until quinoa is desired texture (ie. gooey).
Top with fruit.

Tony's Tip!

Spend the 1-2 minutes to make your meal visually appealing by adding sliced fruit, coconut flakes or nuts.

Healthy Elvis Toast

Serves 1
Ingredients:
1 tablespoon nut butter (natural peanut butter recommended)
1 slice whole wheat whole grain bread or English muffin, toasted
1 banana, sliced
1 tablespoon hemp heart seeds or ground flax
Pinch of cinnamon

Directions:
Spread nut butter on toast.
Assemble banana slices on toast.
Sprinkle with hemp seeds and cinnamon.

> **Tony's Tip!**
>
> Nut butters should only have one ingredient: The nut! No added sugars, fats, or salts.

Bean Purée on Toast

Serves 1
Ingredients:
Bean Purée (page 66–69)
2 slices whole wheat whole grain bread, toasted
Sliced cucumber to cover toast
Sprouts (optional)

Directions:
Liberally spread bean purée on toast.
Add sliced cucumbers and sprouts.

Turkey on Toast with Jalapeño Guacamole

Serves 1
Ingredients:
½ avocado
2 green onions, sliced
1 fresh jalapeño pepper, finely diced, or to taste
½ cup fresh cilantro, chopped
Juice of 1–2 limes
½ teaspoon minced garlic
Pinch of sea salt
Fresh black pepper to taste
1½ ounces low-sodium sliced turkey (about 2 slices)
1 slice whole wheat whole grain bread, toasted

Directions:
Combine avocado, green onions, jalapeño, cilantro, lime juice, garlic, salt and pepper in a bowl. Mix until avocado is well-blended.
Spread mixture on turkey.
Place turkey slices on toast.
Serve as an open-faced sandwich and enjoy!

Toasted Whole Wheat & Hardboiled Eggs

Serves 1
Ingredients:
2 eggs
2 slices whole wheat bread, toasted
Sliced cucumber (optional)

Directions:
Bring water to a boil with eggs in it. Boil 5–8 minutes.
Halve boiled eggs and serve on toast, with cucumbers on the side.

> **Tony's Tip!**
>
> You may wish to use bagels from time to time to add some variety of carbohydrates. Select bagels sparingly.

Southwest Bean & Egg Scramble Wrap

Serves 2
Ingredients:
2 large whole wheat tortillas or wraps
3 medium or large eggs, beaten
½ cup kidney or black beans, washed and rinsed
1 small onion, chopped
½ cup diced green pepper
½ cup diced red pepper
1 tablespoon olive oil
¼ cup cilantro or parsley (optional)
Salsa (optional)

Directions:
Preheat oven to 350°F. Warm whole wheat tortilla in oven for 2–3 minutes.
Heat oil in medium sauté pan over medium heat.
Add onion. Sauté until onion is soft. Mix in peppers and beans and stir for one minute, then pour in eggs. Continue to stir until eggs are cooked.
Divide egg mixture equally into tortilla and top with cilantro or parsley and salsa.

Avocado & Turkey on Toasted Wheat

Serves 1
Ingredients:
1½ ounces low-sodium sliced deli turkey (about 2 slices)
¼ avocado, sliced
1 slice whole wheat whole grain bread, toasted

Directions:
Place turkey slices on toast.
Place avocado slices on turkey.
Serve as an open-faced sandwich and enjoy!

> Tony's Tip!
>
> This goes well with vegetable-based soup.

Bountiful Breakfasts

Egg & Veg Southern Scramble

Serves 2
Ingredients:
1 tablespoon olive or canola oil
8–10 button mushrooms, cleaned and quartered
Pinch of salt
1 medium onion, chopped
½ cup diced red pepper
1½ cup baby spinach
4 medium or large eggs, beaten
Whole wheat tortillas or whole grain whole wheat bread, toasted

Directions:
Heat oil in non-stick sauté pan over medium heat.
Sauté mushrooms until they become slightly brown.
Add pinch of salt, onions and red peppers and cook for 3–4 minutes until onion is soft.
Add spinach and toss in pan until spinach wilts.
Mix in eggs and continue to stir until eggs are cooked.
Serve in whole wheat tortillas or with whole grain whole wheat toast.

Leek Scramble

Serves 2
Ingredients:
4 large eggs, beaten
1 tablespoon olive or canola oil
1 large leek, thinly sliced, cleaned and trimmed
Pinch of salt
Black pepper to taste
Salsa or chopped tomatoes (optional)

Directions:
Heat oil in large sauté pan over medium high heat.
Add leeks, salt and pepper and sauté 3–4 minutes, until leeks are soft.
Tip in eggs and stir until eggs are cooked.
Serve with toast and top with salsa or chopped tomatoes.

34

Indian Spice Tofu Scramble

Serves 2
Ingredients:
1 teaspoon onion powder
1 teaspoon garlic powder
1 teaspoon turmeric
1 teaspoon curry
Pinch of salt
2 teaspoon olive oil
2–3 ounces firm 1" tofu, cut into cubes
Handful fresh spinach

Tony's Tip!

Use cayenne pepper or hot paprika for an extra flare.

Directions:
Combine first five ingredients in small bowl. Set aside.
Heat oil over medium heat using non-stick pan. Add spice blend to oil and stir well.
Add tofu and stir until tofu is coated with spice mixture.
Cook over medium heat until tofu is heated through, approximately 4–6 minutes. Add spinach and stir 1–2 minutes until spinach is wilted.

Oatmeal Pancakes

Serves 2

Ingredients:

1 cup whole wheat flour (substitute buckwheat, quinoa flour or combination of all three)

¾ cup instant or rolled oats

1 tablespoon ground flax

1 tablespoon cinnamon

1 teaspoon baking powder

Pinch of salt

¾ cup buttermilk, plus more if needed

3 eggs, lightly beaten

¾ cup fresh blueberries

Greek yogurt for garnish

Fruit of choice for garnish

Directions:

Preheat electric skillet or griddle to 375°F.

In large bowl, combine flour, oats, flax, cinnamon, baking powder and salt. Mix well. Add in blueberries and set aside.

In medium bowl, combine buttermilk and eggs; blend well.

A bit at a time, add liquid mixture to dry mixture. Stir just until dry ingredients are well combined.

Add more buttermilk if needed.

Ladle pancake batter into hot skillet.

Turn when tops are covered with bubbles and edges look cooked.

Top with fruit of choice or Cherry Compote (page 19).

> **Tony's Tip!**
>
> Add dry ginger into dry mixture for a sweet heat twist.

Veggie Quinoa Frittata

Serves 3
Ingredients:
6 large eggs, beaten
1½ cup cooked quinoa
1–2 medium zucchini, grated
1 large carrot, grated
1 large onion, grated
3 cups spinach or other leafy greens
2 garlic cloves, finely minced
1 tablespoon olive oil
1 teaspoon chili flakes or other seasoning
Salt and black pepper to taste

Directions:

Preheat oven to broil.

Heat oil in large ovenproof, non-stick sauté pan on medium heat. (Ovenproof indicates the entire pan, including the handle, can go into the oven). Add chili flakes to hot oil.

Increase heat to medium high and sauté onions with a pinch of salt until onions are soft and transparent.

Add garlic, carrots and zucchini and cook for 4–6 minutes.

Add spinach or leafy greens and cook until they start to wilt.

Add cooked quinoa.

Mix in beaten eggs with black pepper. Stir in eggs until well incorporated.

Allow eggs to firm slightly, approximately 5–8 minutes.

Place pan on upper rack of oven until eggs are cooked firm, approximately 8–15 minutes. Turn heat off.

Allow to sit in oven for 5–8 minutes.

Remove from oven and flip onto a large serving plate. Be careful: pan is hot.

Luscious Lunches

Many of us have lunch on the run or, worse yet, skip it. With some simple meal planning, lunch does not need to be a chore or take a lot of time to taste great. And an additional bonus of brown-bagging lunch is the money you will save by preparing in advance or assembling at work. I would highly encourage that you disconnect from your desk at lunch, take some "me time" to sit down, relax and enjoy your meal in a mindful way. After all, you are worth it.

Luscious Lunches

Simple Sandwiches =
Protein + Carb + Vegetables

- Select whole grain breads – the kind of bread that goes stale after a few days
- Purchase low-sodium, lean deli meats such as roasted chicken or turkey, packed tuna (packed in water, broth or olive oil) or salmon or use leftovers
- Be sure to load up your sandwich with vegetables such as leafy greens, peppers, tomatoes and cucumbers, etc. Make it a salad between bread

Salads = Vegetables + Protein + Carbohydrate

- Vegetables: Purchase premade salad made up of leafy greens and other vegetables or assemble you own salads
- Protein: Add leftover roasted chicken, turkey, canned tuna, sardines, legumes or hardboiled eggs
- Carb: Choose 2 slices of whole wheat whole grain bread, bun or whole grain crackers such as:

Soups = Protein + Vegetables + Carbohydrate

- Soup: See soup section for easy, tasty recipes that can be prepared in advance (pages 77–96)
- Protein: Choose soups with preferred proteins (chicken, fish or legumes) or have protein on the side for vegetable-based soups
- Carb: Choose 2 slices whole wheat whole grain bread, bun or whole grain crackers as a side to your soup

"Soups are floating salads." — Tony Vassallo, Man on a Nutrition Mission™

Lunch on the Run

Select whole grain pita at Pita Pit or Extreme Pita with lots of veggies.

Salad Bars = Protein + Carb + Vegetables & Fruit

- Protein: Hardboiled eggs, mini-tins of tuna, sardines, legumes, quinoa, low-sodium roasted chicken or turkey from the deli
- Carb: Whole grain kaiser bun or whole grain crackers
- Vegetables and fruit from produce section such as cherry tomatoes, mini carrots, mini cucumber, etc.

Luscious Lunches

Simple Lunch Medley

Serves 1
Ingredients:
1½ ounces Ryvita crackers or Finn Crisp crackers
½ cup tuna or 1–2% cottage cheese
6–7 large olives
As many vegetables as you want!

Directions:
Assemble on plate and enjoy!

Chicken Pita and BIG Salad

Serves 1
Ingredients:
1 medium whole wheat pita
1½ ounces leftover chicken or turkey, warmed in microwave
1 tomato, sliced in wedges
Dijon or plain mustard
Salad made up of lots of veggies

Directions:
Heat pita in microwave or toaster oven.
Place warm chicken on top of pita and tomatoes, dress with mustard.

Tony's Tip!

Load up on vegetables at lunch to help fill you up. This will help with dinner portions and curb cravings later in the day.

Portobello Burger & Shrimp

Serves 1
Ingredients:
1 portobello mushroom
4–5 medium cooked shrimp
1 whole wheat thin burger bun
Lettuce, onion, tomato for burger
Lemon wedges
Side of veggies or greens

> **Tony's Tip!**
>
> Be sure to serve with some protein: shrimp, hard-boiled eggs or cottage cheese work well with this.

Directions:
Gently remove stem from mushroom and use a spoon to scrape black gills from cap. Wipe top of cap with a damp paper towel.
Grill for 3 minutes per side, assemble burger and enjoy with shrimp and lemon on the side.

Egg Salad Wrap

Serves 1
Ingredients:
2 medium or large hardboiled eggs, chopped
1 whole wheat wrap
Shredded lettuce and other vegetables such as sprouts or diced red peppers
Side salad or veggies

Directions:
Assemble eggs and vegetables on wrap or use in a sandwich.
Salad: Serve over bed of greens or sliced tomatoes instead of in wrap.

Spicy Tuna Salad Wrap

Serves 1
Ingredients:
2 ounces water-packed tuna, drained
2 tablespoons horseradish
1–2 tablespoons finely chopped jalapeño pepper
Diced peppers
Green onions
Cilantro or fresh dill (optional)
1 leaf Romaine lettuce (or use whole wheat wrap)
Shredded lettuce

Directions:
Combine first six ingredients. Place tuna mixture on wrap, top with lettuce.

Tuna Salad Sandwich

Serves 1
Ingredients:
2 ounces water-packed tuna, drained
1 teaspoon low-fat mayonnaise or Greek yogurt
Lemon juice (optional)
Chopped green onions
Diced green or red peppers
2 slices whole wheat whole grain bread
Lettuce and tomatoes

Directions:
Mix first five ingredients in small bowl.
Place on tuna mixture on bread and top with lettuce and tomatoes. Enjoy.

Tuna Melt Sandwich

Serves 1
Ingredients:
2 slices whole wheat whole grain bread
1 slice Swiss cheese
2 ounces water-packed tuna, drained
1 medium tomato, sliced
Lettuce or baby spinach

Directions:
Toast bread with cheese in toaster oven.
Top with tuna and veggies.

> Tony's Tip!
>
> Avoid the processed stuff and treat cheese as a condiment.

Salmon Salad Sandwich

Serves 1
Ingredients:
2 ounces water-packed salmon, drained
1–2 teaspoons mayonnaise or Greek yogurt
Chopped green onions
Lemon juice (optional)
2 slices whole wheat whole grain bread
Lettuce and tomatoes

Directions:
Mix salmon, mayonnaise or Greek yogurt, green onions and lemon juice.
Place on bread and top with lettuce and tomatoes. Enjoy.

Lox on Rye

Serves 1
Ingredients:
2 slices whole wheat whole grain or rye bread
2 ounces smoked salmon
Finely sliced red onion
Lettuce
Sliced tomatoes
1 tablespoon capers

Directions:
Assemble sandwich and enjoy.

Crab Salad Wrap

Serves 1
Ingredients:
2 ounces whole crab meat
1–2 teaspoons mayonnaise or horseradish
Lemon or lime juice
Chopped green onions
Sliced celery
Finely diced jalapeño pepper
Lettuce and tomatoes
1 large whole wheat wrap

Directions:
Mix crab meat, mayonnaise or horseradish, lemon juice, green onions, celery and jalapeño. Place on wrap and top with lettuce and tomatoes. Enjoy.

Tony's Tip!

You will find fresh packaged crab in the seafood section of the grocery store. This makes a great alternative to tuna.

Avocado & Tomato on Rye

Serves 1
Ingredients:
¼ avocado, mashed with squeeze of lime or lemon juice
1 slice whole wheat or rye bread
1 thick slice of tomato

Directions:
Spread avocado over bread. Top with tomato slice and enjoy.

Tony's Tip!

This can be used as a perfect snack during long gaps between meals.

Open Boat-Faced Sandwich

Serves 1
Ingredients:
2 slices whole rye
2 slices roasted turkey or chicken
4 large Romaine lettuce leaves
Medley of vegetables
Sprouts
2 slices whole grain bread

Tony's Tip!

Show your creative side and plate your salads with flair.

Directions:
Assemble vegetables inside Romaine lettuce as in picture.
Top with sprouts and serve with side whole grain bread.

Shrimp Martini

Serves 1

Ingredients:

2 ounces cooked shrimp, peeled and de-veined

1 ounce whole wheat crackers

Selection of vegetables

Lemon wedges (optional)

Cocktail sauce (see below)

1 clove garlic, finely minced

Black pepper to taste

Cocktail Sauce

1 tablespoon ketchup

1 teaspoon horseradish

Splash of Tabasco sauce

Directions:

Combine ingredients for cocktail sauce in small bowl.

Boil water in medium pot.

Immerse shrimp in boiling water for 2–3 minutes. Shrimp is cooked when it turns pink and curls. Do not overcook!

Remove shrimp from water. Drain on paper towel to remove any excess moisture.

Drizzle with lemon juice for a citrus twist or toss with finely minced garlic and black pepper.

Plate and enjoy.

Cajun Shrimp: Instead of boiling, toss shrimp with garlic and spices and grill.

Chicken & Veg Pizza

Serves 1
Ingredients:
Sundried tomatoes
1½ ounces cooked chicken (leftovers are great for this)
½ medium red onion, finely sliced
½ cup broccoli florets or finely sliced zucchini
Other vegetables such as red or green peppers, mushrooms, spinach
1 whole wheat whole grain pita

Directions:
Rehydrate tomatoes by immersing dried tomatoes in boiling water. Allow to sit for up to an hour.
Preheat oven 400°F.
Lay all ingredients on pita. Bake in oven for approximately 12–15 minutes.

> ### Tony's Tip!
>
> Substitute sliced hard-boiled eggs, 5% ricotta cheese or goat cheese for chicken for different sources of protein.

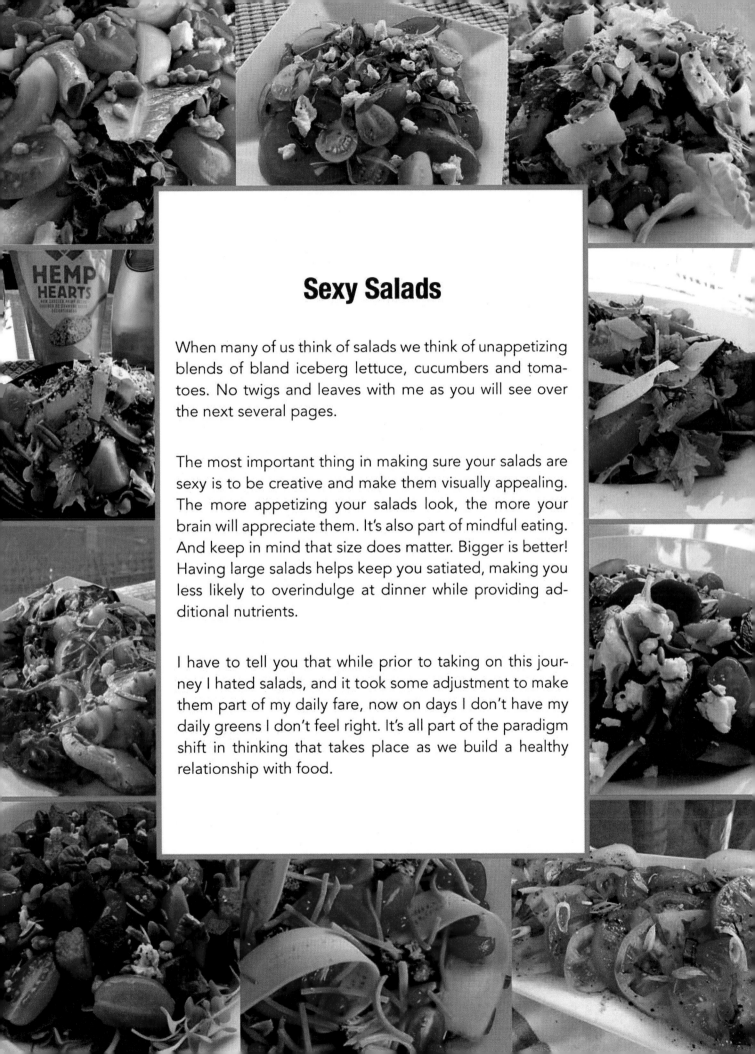

Sexy Salads

When many of us think of salads we think of unappetizing blends of bland iceberg lettuce, cucumbers and tomatoes. No twigs and leaves with me as you will see over the next several pages.

The most important thing in making sure your salads are sexy is to be creative and make them visually appealing. The more appetizing your salads look, the more your brain will appreciate them. It's also part of mindful eating. And keep in mind that size does matter. Bigger is better! Having large salads helps keep you satiated, making you less likely to overindulge at dinner while providing additional nutrients.

I have to tell you that while prior to taking on this journey I hated salads, and it took some adjustment to make them part of my daily fare, now on days I don't have my daily greens I don't feel right. It's all part of the paradigm shift in thinking that takes place as we build a healthy relationship with food.

Tasty Tips To Makes Salads More Nutritious And Delicious

Items To Add To Your Salads:

- Hemp hearts – a great way to add a very nutritious protein to your salads
- Legumes – for some plant-based protein
- Sprouts – when your greens need a little something extra
- Jicama – a cross between a radish and apple
- Avocado – for some healthy dietary fat

Many Fruits Work In Salads:

- Berries (strawberries, raspberries, blueberries and blackberries)
- Sliced or grated apples
- Chopped mango
- Sliced peaches or grilled peaches
- Grapes

Grilled Or Roasted Veggies:

> ### Tony's Tip!
>
> To broil or bake tomatoes, cut Roma tomatoes in half lengthwise. Place on large baking sheet cut side up. Sprinkle with dried or fresh oregano or thyme. Place 3–5 whole garlic cloves on tray. Broil, bake or grill until tomatoes slightly char. Time will vary depending on method or oven. Or you may grill in barbecue basket. Reserve the tomato water for a yummy dressing.
>
> To grill corn, grill raw corn on barbecue until slightly charred. Slice kernels off cob into bowl.

- Grilled zucchini or peppers
- Grilled or roasted onions
- Grilled asparagus
- Grilled mushrooms (portobellos are great for this)
- Grilled or fresh corn kernels
- Broiled or baked tomatoes

Asian Slaw

Makes about 6–7 cups
Ingredients:
3 cups finely shredded green cabbage
2 cups finely shredded red cabbage
1 cup diced cucumber
1 cup grated carrot
2 medium apples, grated and soaked in lemon juice to prevent browning
½ cup unsweetened cranberries
½ cup mint or cilantro (optional)
Fresh black pepper to taste

Slaw Dressing

Lemon juice from apples
⅓ cup seasoned vinegar or apple cider vinegar
2 tablespoons olive or canola oil
1 teaspoon sesame oil
1 teaspoon sugar
¾ teaspoon sea salt or 1 teaspoon celery salt
Fresh black pepper to taste

Directions:
Toss cabbage, cucumber, carrots, apple and cranberries together in large bowl. (Reserve lemon juice from apples. Set aside to be used in dressing recipe.)
Combine all ingredients for dressing in small bowl. Pour over cabbage mixture.
Add mint or cilantro and fresh pepper. Toss until all vegetables are well coated.
Allow to sit for a minimum of 1 hour and up to 48 hours.

> **Tony's Tip!**
>
> Keeps well in refrigerator or serve for pot luck. Adding roasted or grilled onions enhances the flavor of all these dishes.

Fresh Homemade Salsa

Makes 1–1½ cups
Ingredients:
3–4 ripe Roma tomatoes, chopped
½ medium red onion
½ green pepper, diced
1–2 jalapeño, **finely diced**
Juice of 1–2 limes
1–2 tablespoons red wine vinegar
1 tablespoon olive oil
½ cup chopped cilantro or more if desired
Splash of hot sauce (optional)
Salt and fresh pepper to taste

Directions:
Combine ingredients in large bowl. Stir and add hot sauce, if using.

Basic Bean Salad

Serves 8
Ingredients:
1 can (15 ounces) kidney beans, rinsed and drained
1 can (15 ounces) garbanzo beans, rinsed and drained
½ cup chopped red onion
½ cup chopped peppers
¼ cup orange juice or lemon juice
¼ cup cider vinegar or red wine vinegar
4 tablespoons olive oil
Tabasco sauce to taste
1 teaspoon dried oregano
1 clove garlic, finely chopped or use 1 teaspoon garlic purée
Salt and pepper to taste

Directions:
In a bowl, gently mix the beans and onions until well combined.
In a separate bowl, whisk together the liquid ingredients, oregano and garlic.
Pour the liquid mixture over the beans. Stir to coat evenly. Let stand 30 minutes before serving.
Note: You may wish to substitute any beans you choose.

Tony's Tip!

Legumes are an overlooked protein source. They are a true powerhouse protein as they contain fiber plus lots of other healthy nutrients. Not to mention our microbes love them too.

Quinoa and Egg Salad

Serves 1
Ingredients:
1 cup cooked quinoa
2 large eggs, hardboiled and chopped
Pinch of salt
Fresh black pepper
Chopped green onion (optional)
¼ avocado, sliced

Directions:
Combine all ingredients except avocado. Place sliced avocado on top.
Serve warm or cold.

Tony's Tip!

Combine any other veggies such as peppers, cucumber, tomatoes as you wish. Quinoa salads were my favorite lunch or snack ideas.

Super Veg Salad

Ingredients:
Baby greens
Cooked or raw broccoli
Tomatoes, quartered or sliced
Red onion, thinly sliced
Carrot or cucumber curls

Tony's Tip!

Use a good quality vegetable peeler to make carrot curls. It works with cucumber and zucchini too.

Super Veg Salad with Berries

Ingredients:
Chopped and washed romaine lettuce
Cooked or raw broccoli
Cherry or grape tomatoes, halved
Carrot, cut into matchsticks
Berries or currants
Yellow zucchini curls

Veggie Salad

Ingredients:
Baby greens
Tomatoes
Yellow peppers
Grated carrots
Radish slices
Green beans

Wild Salad

Ingredients:
Baby spinach greens or any other baby green
Zucchini curls
Cherry tomatoes
Cucumber
Grilled or fresh peach quarters
Sliced mushrooms
Fresh cracked black pepper
Sprouts (optional)
Hemp seeds or hearts (optional)

Chef Salad with Fruit

Ingredients:
Baby greens
Cherry tomatoes
Red pepper
Cucumber, chopped
Mushrooms
Radishes
Baby spinach
Peach slices
Variant: Substitute sliced apples soaked in lemon juice instead of peaches

Tomato Salad

Ingredients:
Tomato medley, sliced
Fresh basil, chopped
Goat cheese, sliced or crumbled
Red onion slices
Balsamic vinegar

Directions:
Top tomatoes with basil, cheese and onion. Drizzle vinegar over salad.

Creamy Celery Cucumber & Fennel Salad

Serves 4
Ingredients:
½ cup plain Greek yogurt
2 tablespoons cider or rice wine vinegar
1 teaspoon finely minced garlic or use garlic purée
1 fennel bulb, core removed, finely sliced (reserve fronds for garnish)
1 cup sliced celery or more if desired
1 cup sliced cucumber or more if desired
¼ cup fresh dill
Fresh black pepper
½ teaspoon salt (optional)

Directions:
Whisk together yogurt, vinegar and garlic.
Toss in fennel, celery, cucumber, dill, pepper and salt.
Allow to marinate for 1–4 hours.
Garnish with fennel fronds.

Grilled Caesar Salad

Serves 4
Ingredients:
2 tablespoons olive oil
3 tablespoons Dijon mustard
3 tablespoons red wine vinegar
3 tablespoons lemon juice + 1 teaspoon lemon zest
1–2 garlic cloves, finely minced
1 teaspoon anchovy paste
2 romaine lettuce hearts, halved and cleaned
½ cup feta cheese
Fresh black pepper to taste

Directions:
Preheat grill to medium heat.
Whisk together olive oil, mustard, vinegar, lemon juice, garlic, lemon zest and anchovy paste.
Grill lettuce hearts, cut side down and covered, for 1–3 minutes until lettuce just begins to wilt.
Remove from grill and place on platter.
Drizzle dressing over halved romaine hearts.
Crumble feta over warm lettuce, add black pepper.

> Tony's Tip!
>
> Feel free to grill up extra veggies to top your salad.

Moroccan Bean & Potato Salad

Serves 4
Ingredients:
4 medium russet potatoes, washed and cut into 2" chunks
1–2 tablespoons olive oil
1 large onion, diced
1 tablespoon grated fresh ginger
1 teaspoon ground cumin
½ teaspoon cinnamon
¼ teaspoon ground coriander
1 leek, sliced and cleaned
1 cup diced carrots
¾ cup sliced celery
1 can (14 ounces) diced tomatoes
Fresh black pepper to taste
Juice of 1 lemon
Chopped parsley
1 can (28 ounces) garbanzo or red kidney beans, rinsed and drained

Directions:
Cook potatoes in boiling water until soft, about 20 minutes.
Drain potatoes and set aside.
Heat oil over medium heat in large sauté pan or Dutch oven. Add onions and spices, mix well.
Cook until onions slightly soften, about 2–4 minutes.
Add leeks, carrots and celery, stir. Cook for 3–4 minutes.
Add tomatoes, beans and potatoes, stir and allow potatoes to break apart.
Reduce heat to medium low, cook covered until warm.
Season with fresh black pepper.
When ready to serve garnish with lemon juice and parsley.

> Tony's Tip!
>
> When it comes to salads the more veggies the better!

Spreads & Dressings

With dressings, there is this notion that they have got to be on the side – no need for any of that diet mentality here but use caution. Avoid store-bought dressings; most are sugar combined with highly processed oils. Instead, make your own.

Garbanzo Bean and Roasted Pepper Purée

Makes 1½ cups
Ingredients:
1 can (14 ounces) garbanzo beans, rinsed
1 tablespoon tahini or olive oil
3–4 roasted red peppers
Juice of one lemon
Black pepper to taste
1 jalapeño, finely diced

Directions:
Combine garbanzo beans, roasted red pepper, lemon juice and pepper.
Purée using an immersion blender until well blended.
Mix in diced jalapeño.
Serve with veggies.

Chunky Black Bean & Tomato Spread

Makes about 1½ cups
Ingredients:
1 can (14 ounces) black beans, rinsed
2–3 teaspoon olive oil
1–2 shallots, finely chopped
2 tablespoons tomato paste
1 tablespoon Dijon mustard
1–2 tablespoons red wine vinegar
1 teaspoon chili flakes (optional)
Black pepper to taste

Directions:
Heat oil in heavy, medium saucepan.
Add shallots, cook 3–4 minutes until shallots are soft.
Stir in tomato paste.
Add remaining ingredients, stirring constantly, until well blended.
Cook until beans break and become soft, about 6–8 minutes.
Transfer to bowl and set aside to cool.

Roasted Fennel Veg & Kidney Bean Purée with Jalapeño

Makes about 6–7 cups
Ingredients:
1 medium to large sweet onion, cut into eighths
2 medium carrots in 1" slices
1 can (14 ounces) red kidney beans, rinsed
2 jalapeño pepper, diced
1 tablespoon olive oil (optional)
1 teaspoon fennel seeds
Pinch of salt
Black pepper to taste

Directions:
Preheat oven to 400°F. Toss onions and carrots with fennel seeds, olive oil, salt and pepper in large baking dish lined with tinfoil. Be sure to spread evenly. If making a large batch you may need to bake in two batches.
Roast in oven for 35–45 minutes or until vegetables are soft and slightly caramelized. Mix once while roasting to avoid sticking. Turn off heat. Allow to sit until cool, 30–40 minutes.
Combine roasted vegetables with kidney beans in deep bowl. Purée with immersion blender to make a paste. Stir in diced jalapeño.
Set aside to cool.

> **Tony's Tip!**
>
> This can be used as a spread for sandwiches or as a side. Add roasted garlic to any legume or vegetable dip or spread for extra flavor.

Fresh Homemade Guacamole

Makes 1–1½ cups
Ingredients:
1 avocado
1 jalapeño pepper, finely chopped
1 small to medium red onion, diced
Juice of 1–2 limes
½ cup chopped fresh cilantro
Pinch of salt
Minced garlic (optional)

Directions:
Mash avocado in large bowl. Stir in remaining ingredients.

Spreads and Dressings

Lentil Spread

Makes 1 cup
Ingredients:
1 cup cooked or canned lentils, rinsed
Juice of 2–3 lemons or 3–4 limes + zest of ½ lemon or 1 lime
2–3 cloves chopped garlic
1 tablespoon tahini or olive oil
Cayenne pepper (optional)
Black pepper to taste

Directions:
Combine all ingredients in a deep bowl.
Purée with immersion blender.

> **Tony's Tip!**
>
> Adding roasted or grilled onions enhances the flavor of this dish.

Red Bean Spread

Makes 1½ cups
Ingredients:
1 can (14 ounces) red kidney beans, rinsed
1–2 tablespoons olive oil
2–3 shallots or 1 medium onion, finely chopped
1 teaspoon chili flakes
2 tablespoons chicken stock or vegetable stock (or more if needed)
Black pepper to taste

Directions:
Heat oil in heavy saucepan over medium heat. Add shallots and chili flakes. Stir until shallots are soft and translucent.
Stir in beans, reduce heat to low and cook for 5 minutes, stirring occasionally.
Take mixture off heat and stir in chicken stock using immersion blender or transfer to a stand up blender to make a paste.
Transfer to bowl and set aside to cool.

> **Tony's Tip!**
>
> This can be used as a dip or spread liberally on toast or whole wheat crackers as a source of protein for a meal.

Garlic & Shallot White Bean Dip

Makes 2 cups
Ingredients:
1 (14 ounces) can white beans (cannellini or navy work well with this)
2–3 garlic cloves, crushed
1–2 shallots, finely chopped
1 tablespoon olive oil
Juice of 1–2 medium lemons
Zest of half a lemon
Black or white pepper to taste

Directions:
Purée all ingredients in a large bowl using immersion blender.
Serve warm or refrigerate and use later.

Cranberry Chutney

Makes 1 cup
Ingredients:
½ bag (6–7 ounces) fresh or frozen cranberries
2 shallots, finely minced
Rind of one orange, finely minced
Juice of two oranges
1 teaspoon olive oil
Freshly chopped sage
Cayenne pepper
2–3 teaspoons sugar (optional)
Pinch of salt

> ### Tony's Tip!
>
> This cranberry chutney is a great, healthy alternative with roasted poultry.

Directions:
Heat olive oil over low to medium heat in medium saucepan.
Increase heat to medium high, add shallots, salt, orange rind, chopped sage and cayenne.
Sweat for 2–3 minutes until shallots are soft.
Add sugar, deglaze using orange juice and simmer until liquid reduces by half.
Reduce heat to medium low, add cranberries and stir until berries liquify.

Spreads and Dressings

Light Version of Citrus Italian Vinaigrette

Serves 3–4
Ingredients:
4 tablespoons lemon or lime juice
2 tablespoons extra virgin olive oil
1 garlic clove, crushed or 1 shallot, chopped
1 teaspoon fresh or dried oregano
½ teaspoon finely chopped zest of lemon (optional)
Salt and pepper to taste

Directions:
Combine all ingredients in sealable jar such as a mason jar.
Close and shake vigorously.
Refrigerate before serving.

Tony's Tip!

Make a large batch of dressing and store in mason jars in the refrigerator. Like some heat in your dressing? Add a squeeze of sriracha sauce.

If you don't have time to make a dressing, use good-quality balsamic vinegar or fruit-based vinegar.

Zesty Citrus Italian Vinaigrette

Serves 3–4
Ingredients:
4 tablespoons lemon or lime juice
2 tablespoons extra virgin olive oil
1 teaspoon crushed chili flakes or Tabasco sauce
1 teaspoon fresh or dried oregano (optional)
½ teaspoon finely chopped zest of lemon (optional)
Pinch salt (optional)
Black pepper as desired

Directions:
Combine all ingredients in sealable jar such as a mason jar.
Close and shake vigorously.
Refrigerate before serving.

Light Version of Balsamic Italian Vinaigrette

Serves 3–4
Ingredients:
4 tablespoons quality balsamic vinegar
2 tablespoons extra virgin olive oil
1–2 crushed garlic cloves
1 teaspoon fresh or dried oregano
½ teaspoon finely chopped zest of lemon
Black pepper as desired
Pinch of salt

Directions:
Whisk ingredients together. Refrigerate before serving.

Asian Vinaigrette

Serves 3–4
Ingredients:
¼ cup rice wine vinegar
1 tablespoon canola oil or grapeseed oil (choose neutral-tasting unsaturated oil)
1 teaspoon low-sodium soy sauce
1 teaspoon minced fresh ginger
½ teaspoon sesame oil

Directions:
Whisk ingredients together.

Citrus Asian Vinaigrette

Serves 3–4
Ingredients:
Juice of 1–2 limes
¼ cup rice wine vinegar
1 tablespoon canola oil or grape seed oil (choose neutral-tasting unsaturated oil)
1 teaspoon low-sodium soy sauce
1 teaspoon lime zest
1 teaspoon minced ginger
½ teaspoon sesame oil

Directions:
Whisk ingredients together.

Spreads and Dressings

Spicy Vinaigrette

Serves 3–4
Ingredients:
1–2 tablespoons sriracha sauce
¼ cup low-sodium rice wine vinegar
1 garlic clove, finely minced or 1 teaspoon garlic or ginger powder
Pinch of cayenne or black pepper (optional)

Directions:
Whisk ingredients together.

Mustard Vinaigrette

Tony's Tip!

Mustard makes a great emulsifier while adding next to no calories and enhances flavor. Use mustard in place of oil for almost any dressing.

Serves 5–6
Ingredients:
4–5 tablespoons Dijon mustard
4–5 tablespoons white wine vinegar
½ teaspoon mustard powder
Pinch of cayenne pepper

Directions:
Whisk ingredients together. Refrigerate before serving.

Roasted Red Pepper Balsamic Pesto

Serves 12+
Ingredients:
4–6 roasted peppers (homemade or vinegar-based jar)

½ cup balsamic or red wine vinegar
1 garlic clove, finely minced
Pinch of cayenne or black pepper (optional)
Sriracha sauce to taste (optional)

Tony's Tip!

This makes great leftovers. Make a big batch and freeze. Roasted veggies add a rich healthy flavor to any soup.

Directions:
Place ingredients in blender. Blend until smooth.
Transfer to glass jar or bowl and cover.
Refrigerate until serving.

Avocado Dressing

Serves 4–6
Ingredients:
1 small ripe avocado
Juice of 2 limes
1 finely minced garlic (optional)

Directions:
Split avocado, remove pit. Scoop out flesh. Mash avocado. Whisk remaining ingredients together.

Spicy Avocado Dressing

Serves 4–6
Ingredients:
1 small ripe avocado
Juice of 2 limes
Pinch of cayenne or black pepper
1 teaspoon sriracha sauce

Directions:
Split avocado, remove pit. Scoop out flesh. Mash avocado. Whisk remaining ingredients together.

Green Tea Avocado Mayo

Serves 4–6
Ingredients:
1 medium ripe avocado
½ cup green tea, room temperature
2–3 heaping tablespoons unflavored Greek yogurt
Juice of 1 lemon
Pinch of salt
Pinch of cayenne pepper

Directions:
Prepare as above.

Tony's Tip!

This makes a great dressing for a potato salad.

Basic Mango Mustard Dressing

Serves 6–8

Ingredients:

1 cup diced ripe mango

⅓ cup cider vinegar or more if needed

Directions:

Place ingredients in blender. Blend until smooth.

Transfer to glass jar or bowl and cover.

Refrigerate until serving.

> ### Tony's Tip!
>
> These tropical dressings may seem unusual, however they make for great vinaigrette or as a sauce for chicken, fish or pork. If you have an immersion blender, you can blend them right in the serving bowl.

Spicy Mango Mustard Dressing

Serves 6–8

Ingredients:

1 cup diced ripe mango

⅓ cup cider vinegar or more if needed

1–2 teaspoons chili flakes or hot sauce

1 teaspoon mustard powder (optional)

Directions:

Place ingredients in blender. Blend until smooth.

Transfer to glass jar or bowl and cover.

Refrigerate until serving.

Creamy Fruit Dressing

Serves 6–8

Ingredients:

1 cup diced ripe mango, papaya or pineapple

⅓ cup apple cider vinegar or more if needed

2–4 heaping tablespoons 0% Greek yogurt

Black pepper as desired or chili flakes (optional)

> ### Tony's Tip!
>
> This makes a great dressing for a potato salad. You can even add the papaya seeds into the mix.

Directions:

Place ingredients in blender. Blend until smooth.

Transfer to glass jar or bowl and cover.

Refrigerate until serving.

Succulent Soups

Soups were a winter staple while I was losing my weight. They gave me an opportunity to spend some time in the kitchen with youthful tunes in the background. Many times I opened up the refrigerator to find creative combinations of veggies mixed in with legumes and lentils. I encourage you to mix and match veggies, spices and herbs to come up with your own favorites. Make large batches as they make great lunches and most freeze well.

Succulent Soups

Simple Tomato Soup

Tony's Tip!

This makes a great evening supper in the winter. Serve in large mug and sip away while reading a great book on a cold winter's night.

Serves 2
Ingredients:
1 cup strained tomatoes
1½ cups no-salt chicken stock
1–2 garlic cloves, finely minced
Fresh basil, for garnish
Balsamic vinegar, for garnish

Directions:
Combine strained tomatoes and stock in saucepan. Add garlic.
Warm on medium heat.
Garnish with torn fresh basil and drizzle with balsamic vinegar.

Simple Pumpkin Soup

Serves 2
Ingredients:
1 can (about 14 ounces) pumpkin purée
2 cups no-salt chicken stock or more if desired
Fresh nutmeg, grated

Directions:
Combine pumpkin purée and stock in saucepan.
Add grated nutmeg.
Warm on medium heat.
Garnish with more fresh nutmeg or diced apples.

Tony's Tip!

Add teff to this dish and you have a complete breakfast or lunch.

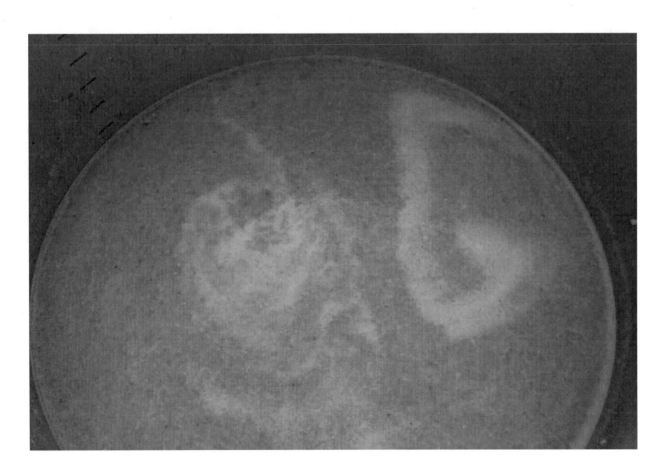

Split Pea Soup

Serves 4

Ingredients:

1 tablespoon olive or canola oil

1 large Spanish onion, chopped

1 teaspoon dried oregano or thyme

1 teaspoon black pepper

Salt to taste

1 cup chopped carrots

1 cup diced celery

1–2 cloves garlic, finely chopped

1½ cups dried green split peas

6 cups low-sodium chicken or vegetable stock

Directions:

Warm oil in large sauce or soup pot over medium heat. Add onions and herbs and sauté until soft, about 4–5 minutes.

Add carrots, celery and garlic, stir. Reduce heat.

Mix in split peas and stir to combine.

Increase heat to medium high. Add stock, stir and cover.

Bring to a slow boil.

Simmer uncovered for 30–40 minutes or until peas are cooked and soft.

Blend with immersion blender or leave chunky.

Lentil Tomato & Greens Soup

Serves 4

Ingredients:

1–2 tablespoons olive oil

1 large Spanish onion, chopped

1½ teaspoons dried oregano or thyme

1 teaspoon black pepper

1–2 cloves garlic, finely chopped

1 cup chopped carrots

1 cup diced celery

1½ cups green, brown or red lentils

1 can (19 ounces) Roma tomatoes, with liquid

6 cups low-sodium chicken or vegetable stock

1–2 cup fresh or frozen spinach or kale

Tony's Tip!

Always be sure to have items such as puréed tomatoes and low- or no-salt stock in your pantry.

Directions:

Heat oil in large sauce or soup pot over medium heat.

Add onions and herbs. Sauté until onions are soft, about 4–5 minutes.

Add garlic, celery and carrots, stir.

Reduce heat. Mix in lentils and stir to combine.

Add tomatoes with liquid and stir.

Increase heat to medium high. Pour in stock, stir and cover.

Bring to a slow boil.

Simmer uncovered for 30 minutes or until lentils are cooked and soft.

Add spinach or kale, turn off heat.

Simple Carrot Soup

Serves 4–6
Ingredients:
1–2 tablespoons olive or canola oil
1 large Spanish onion, chopped
1 garlic clove, finely minced
½ teaspoon fresh ground nutmeg (optional)
Freshly ground pepper
1 cup diced celery or more if desired
5–6 medium carrots, chopped
6 cups low-sodium chicken or vegetable stock
¼ teaspoon salt (optional)
Fresh dill, toasted sunflower seeds or toasted coconut for garnish

Directions:
Warm oil in a large sauce or soup pot over medium heat.
Add onions and sauté until soft, about 4–5 minutes.
Stir in garlic, nutmeg and pepper.
Add celery and half of the carrots and stir. Cook for 1–3 minutes.
Add remaining carrots.
Pour in stock, stir and cover.
Increase heat to medium high and bring soup to a slow boil.
Simmer uncovered for 30–40 minutes or until carrots are soft.
Blend with immersion blender.
Serve cold or warm and garnish with fresh dill, toasted sunflower seeds and coconut.

Roasted Pepper Soup

Serves 4–6
Ingredients:
1 tablespoon olive or canola oil
1 large Spanish onion, chopped
1 garlic clove, finely minced
2–3 medium carrots, chopped
1 cup diced celery
1 tablespoon hot or sweet paprika
8 roasted red peppers (store-bought or make your own – see page 84)
4 cups low-sodium chicken or vegetable stock
2 bay leaves

Fresh black pepper to taste
Fresh chives (optional)

Directions:
Warm oil in large sauce or soup pot over medium heat.
Add onions and sauté until soft, about 4–5 minutes. Add garlic, carrots and celery and stir. Cook for 2–3 minutes.
Add paprika, stir and cook 1–2 minutes.
Add roasted peppers, stir and cook 1–2 minutes.
Add stock and bay leaves and stir while increasing heat to medium high. Cover and bring to a slow boil.
Simmer uncovered for 15–20 minutes or until vegetables are soft or desired texture.
Remove bay leaves.
Purée with an immersion blender.
Serve cold or warm and garnish with fresh chives.

Roasted Red Pepper and Tomato Soup

Serves 4
Ingredients:
6–7 large red bell peppers
8 large Roma tomatoes, cut in half cross-wise
4–5 large garlic cloves
1 large onion (quartered)
1–2 tablespoons olive oil
4 cups low-sodium chicken or vegetable stock
Salt and pepper to taste
Balsamic vinegar

Directions:
Preheat oven to 425°F.
Place vegetables onto a tinfoil-lined baking dish.
Drizzle olive oil over vegetables and toss to coat.
Place peppers and tomatoes cut sides down. Bake for 45–60 minutes, until the peppers and tomatoes darken and wilt.
Remove pan from oven and let cool. Once cool, remove skins from peppers and tomatoes.
Place all vegetables into a medium to large soup pot.
Add stock and bring to a slow boil over medium high heat.
Simmer uncovered for about 15 minutes.
Purée with blender or leave chunky.
Season salt and pepper to taste.
Drizzle each bowl with balsamic vinegar.

Chicken Vegetable Soup

Serves 4

Ingredients:

6 cups low-sodium chicken stock
1 pound chicken breast
1 tablespoon olive or canola oil
1 large Spanish onion, chopped
1 leek, cleaned and finely chopped
1–2 garlic cloves, finely chopped
1 teaspoon dried oregano
1 teaspoon black pepper
1 cup chopped carrots
1 cup diced celery
1–2 tablespoons finely chopped flat leaf parsley

Directions:

Bring stock to a simmer in a medium to large saucepan over medium high heat.

Add chicken breast and simmer until chicken is tender, about 12–15 minutes.

Cool stock with chicken submerged in soup.

Remove chicken from stock and chop or pull by hand into bite-size pieces. Set aside.

In separate large saucepan, heat oil over medium heat. Add onions and sauté until onions soften slightly.

Add leeks, garlic, oregano, black pepper and cook for 2–3 minutes.

Add carrots and celery, cook, stirring, for 3–4 minutes.

Tip in reserved chicken, stir for 1–2 minutes.

Increase heat to high.

Pour stock into vegetable and chicken mixture and stir.

Bring to boil then reduce heat to low. Cook until vegetables are desired texture, about 8–10 minutes.

Serve or set aside.

Top with parsley.

> Tony's Tip!
>
> Add other vegetables such as zucchini, green beans, cauliflower etc. No need to thaw if using frozen chicken breasts. You can simmer from frozen.

Minestra (Minestrone Soup)

Serves 6–8

Ingredients:

2 tablespoons olive or canola oil

1 large Spanish onion, diced

¼ teaspoon salt

1 teaspoon chili flakes

1 teaspoon dried oregano

1–2 leeks, finely chopped

2–4 garlic cloves, finely minced

1½ cup diced carrot

1 cup sliced celery

1 can (about 15 ounces) diced tomatoes, with liquid strained and reserved

1 cup pot barley, rinsed

8 cups low-sodium chicken or vegetable stock

1 can (about 15 ounces) red kidney beans or beans of choice

2 cups chopped savoy cabbage or kale

Fresh black pepper to taste

> ### Tony's Tip!
>
> Minestrone soup is a classic vegetable soup that combines whatever veggies you have on hand with legumes.

Directions:

Warm oil in a large soup pot over medium high heat.

Add onions, salt and chili flakes and sauté for 2–3 minutes.

Add oregano, leeks and garlic and stir for 2–4 minutes.

Reduce heat to medium and cook until onions and leeks soften slightly.

Increase heat to medium high, add carrots and celery and sauté for 3–5 minutes.

Add tomatoes without the liquid. Increase heat to high, stir for 3–4 minutes. Add stock and reserved tomato liquid.

Cover and bring to a boil. Lower heat and simmer for 30 minutes.

Add barley. Cook covered until barley is soft, about 25–35 minutes.

Add beans and cabbage. Turn off heat and allow to sit for 30 minutes, stirring occasionally.

Serve warm or refrigerate or freeze.

Turkey Vegetable Chili Stew

Serves 6
Ingredients:
1 pound lean ground turkey or chicken
3–5 garlic cloves, finely chopped
2 tablespoons olive oil
2 cups chopped onion
1½ cups chopped carrots
1½ cups diced celery
1 can (28 ounces) diced tomatoes
1½ cups low-sodium vegetable or low-sodium chicken broth
1 can (19 ounces) red kidney beans, well rinsed and drained
1 can (19 ounces) white kidney beans or black beans, well rinsed and drained
1 green pepper, coarsely chopped
8 ounces button mushrooms, cleaned and quartered
2 cups chopped fresh spinach or 10-ounce package frozen spinach or kale
1 cup corn

Homemade Chili Powder Blend

Ingredients:
2 teaspoons ground cumin
2 teaspoons paprika
1½ teaspoons cayenne pepper
1 teaspoon ground pepper
1 teaspoon garlic powder
½ teaspoon dried oregano
½ teaspoon salt

Directions:
Combine all spices for chili powder in small bowl. Set aside.

Sauté half the ground poultry meat in a large heavy-bottomed soup pot or Dutch oven over medium high heat until meat is brown. Sprinkle one quarter of the chili powder blend. Drain and set aside.

Sauté the remaining ground poultry meat, sprinkle one quarter of the spice blend. Set cooked ground meat aside; toss half chopped garlic into meat to infuse with garlic flavor.

Add oil to pot, add all onions and sauté for 3–4 minutes. Reduce heat to medium. Add remaining spice blend, garlic and half the carrots and celery. Cook for 2–3 minutes until fragrant.

Add remaining carrots and celery, cook for 2–3 minutes. Add half of the cooked ground poultry meat. Cook for 3–4 minutes, add remaining ground meat. Cook for 2–3 minutes, add chopped tomatoes with liquid and stock. Stir, cover and bring to slow boil.
Add beans, green peppers and mushrooms, lower heat to simmer.
Let simmer for 30–45 minutes.
Add spinach or kale, corn, turn off and allow to sit or serve immediately.

Curried Creamy Parsnip & Butter Bean Soup

Serves 2–4
Ingredients:
1 tablespoon olive oil
1 large Spanish onion, chopped
2–3 garlic cloves, finely minced
¼ teaspoon salt
2 tablespoons curry powder
1 pound parsnips, chopped
4–5 cups low-sodium chicken or vegetable stock
1 can (14 ounces) butter beans, drained and rinsed
¼–½ cup buttermilk
Chives, chopped

Fresh black pepper to taste
Hot sauce (optional)

Directions:
Heat oil on medium heat in heavy-bottomed soup pot or Dutch oven.
Add onions, garlic and salt. Sauté for 5 minutes. Add curry powder.
Stir until aromatic and onions are soft.
Add parsnips, stock and beans.
Cover, increase heat to medium high and bring to a boil.
Simmer on low for 30–40 minutes. Parsnips should be soft.
Blend mixture using immersion blender. Add buttermilk.
Heat and serve with chopped chives and fresh cracked black pepper and drizzle with hot sauce.

> **Tony's Tip!**
>
> Try roasting the parsnips for a more gourmet version of this soup.

Moroccan Lentil and Carrot Soup with a Hint of Apricots

Serves 6

Ingredients:

1½ teaspoons ground cumin

1½ teaspoons ground coriander

1 teaspoon ground turmeric

1 teaspoon ground fennel seed

1 teaspoon ground black pepper

½ teaspoon garlic powder

½ teaspoon curry powder

½ teaspoon salt

2 tablespoons olive oil

1–1 ½ cups chopped onions

1 cups chopped carrots

1 cups diced celery

3–4 garlic cloves, finely chopped

2 tablespoons tomato paste

½ cup Turkish apricots, finely diced

1½ cups lentils, split peas or combination, rinsed

3–4 cups of low-sodium chicken or vegetable stock (more if needed)

Lemons or limes (optional)

> **Tony's Tip!**
>
> This version of Moroccan soup is my all-time favorite soup.

Directions:

Combine all spices in small bowl and set aside.

Heat oil in a heavy-bottomed soup pot or Dutch oven over medium high heat.

Add onions and sauté for 2–3 minutes. Reduce heat to medium.

Add one third of spice mixture. Cook for 1–2 minutes until fragrant.

Stir in half of carrots, celery and garlic with another third of spice combination. Cook for 2–4 minutes.

Add remaining spices, carrots, celery and garlic. Continue to stir until onions are soft. Reduce heat to medium low.

Add apricots and cook for 1–2 minutes. Stir in lentils or split peas in thirds until well coated with spices, stirring for 2–4 minutes each time. Add stock.

Cover, bring to boil over medium high heat. Reduce to low. Simmer for 35–45 minutes or until lentils and split peas have reached desired texture.

Purée with immersion blender for smooth consistency or leave chunky.

Squeeze in lemon or lime when ready to serve.

Moroccan Lentil and Vegetable Soup

Serves 6–8
Ingredients:
1 teaspoon ground cumin
1 teaspoon ground coriander
1 teaspoon ground turmeric
1 teaspoon ground fennel seed
1 teaspoon ground pepper
½ teaspoon garlic powder
½ teaspoon curry powder
½ teaspoon salt
¼ teaspoon ground cinnamon
2 tablespoons olive oil
1½ cups chopped onions
1 cup chopped carrots
1 cup diced celery
2–3 garlic cloves, finely chopped

1 tablespoon tomato paste
1 can (28 ounces) diced tomatoes
2 cups lentils, split peas or combination, rinsed
8 cups low-sodium vegetable or chicken broth
2 cups chopped cauliflower florets
2–3 cups chopped fresh spinach or 10-ounce package frozen chopped spinach
Lemons or limes (optional)

Directions:
Combine all spices. Set aside.
Heat oil in a large heavy-bottomed soup pot over medium high heat. Add onions, sauté for 2–3 minutes. Reduce heat to medium.
Add one third of spice mixture. Cook for 1–2 minutes until fragrant.
Stir in half of carrots, celery and garlic with another third of spice combination. Cook for 2–4 minutes.
Add remaining carrots, celery, garlic, spices and tomato paste. Continue to stir until onions are soft. Reduce heat to medium low.
Stir in tomatoes, cook for 1–2 minutes.
Add lentils or split peas in one third batches. Cook and stir each batch for 4–5 minutes.
Add stock. Cover, bring to slow boil. Reduce high to low. Simmer for 35–45 minutes or until lentils and split peas have reached desired texture.
Add cauliflower, cook uncovered for 4–5 minutes.
Turn off heat, add spinach or kale. Stir until greens wilt.
Just before serving, squeeze lemon or lime juice into soup.

Caribbean Curried Pumpkin Soup

Serves 2–4

Ingredients:

1–2 tablespoons olive oil

1 large Spanish onion, chopped, or 2 leeks (white part only), finely chopped

2–3 garlic cloves, finely minced

2 tablespoons curry powder

2 cups pumpkin purée

4 cups low-sodium chicken or vegetable stock

¾ cup unsweetened coconut milk

Fresh nutmeg to taste

Directions:

Heat oil on medium heat in a heavy-bottomed soup pot or Dutch oven.

Add onions and sauté for 2–3 minutes.

Add garlic and curry powder. Stir until aromatic and onions are soft.

Reduce heat to medium low.

Pour in pumpkin purée, stir.

Increase to medium high heat, cook for 4–6 minutes.

Add stock, stir, cover, increase heat and bring to a slow boil.

Reduce heat to a simmer for 25–35 minutes.

Blend mixture using immersion blender.

Stir in coconut milk. Serve warm with fresh nutmeg on top.

Tony's Tip!

Sprinkle corn kernels and pumpkin seeds into this or other soups for color and a burst of healthy sweetness.

Asian Carrot Soup

Serves 4–6
Ingredients:
1 tablespoon olive or canola oil
2 leeks, trimmed, cleaned and chopped
1–2 teaspoons fresh ginger, finely minced
1–2 teaspoons orange zest or more if desired, finely grated
Pinch of salt
Fresh black pepper to taste
1 cup diced celery or more if desired
5 medium carrots, chopped
Juice from 1–2 oranges
6 cups low-sodium chicken or vegetable stock
1 teaspoon sesame oil
Orange slices for garnish
Fresh mint or dill for garnish

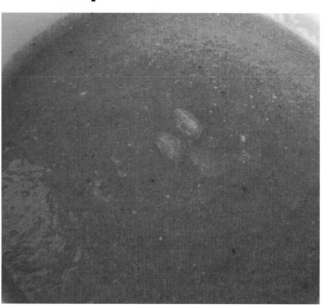

Directions:
Warm olive oil in a large soup pot over medium heat.
Add leeks and sauté until soft for 4–5 minutes.
Stir in ginger, orange zest, salt and pepper.
Add celery and half of carrots and cook, stirring, for 1–3 minutes.
Add remaining carrots and cook for 1–3 minutes.
Pour in orange juice and stock, stir and cover.

Increase heat to medium high and bring to a slow boil.
Simmer uncovered for 30–40 minutes or until carrots are soft or desired texture.
Blend with immersion blender.
Serve cold or warm. Drizzle sesame oil in soup just before serving.
Garnish with orange slices and mint or dill.

Mushroom Medley Soup

Serves 4

Ingredients:

1 tablespoon olive oil

2 teaspoons sesame oil

1 medium leek, cleaned and chopped (optional)

4–5 cups chopped mushrooms (button, shiitake, oyster, portobello, etc.), wiped with damp paper towel remove any dirt residue

1 tablespoon dried oregano

1–2 cloves garlic, finely minced

Fresh black pepper to taste

4–5 cups low-sodium chicken or vegetable stock

3 green onions, chopped on bias

Directions:

Heat large soup pot or enamel pot over medium heat and add olive and sesame oils.

Add leeks and sweat until soft, about 4–6 minutes.

Add mushrooms, oregano, garlic and black pepper, mix until mushrooms are coated. You may need to add mushroom in two batches.

Cook until mushrooms are soft.

Increase heat to high, add stock. Cover and bring to a boil.

Reduce heat to medium low and cook uncovered for 15 minutes.

Set aside until ready to serve.

Garnish with green onions.

> **Tony's Tip!**
>
> Toast whole grain pita until crispy. They make a great substitution for crackers for soup.

Roasted Acorn Squash & Apple Soup

Serves 6
Ingredients:
1 large acorn squash
1 tablespoon olive or canola oil
2 leeks, trimmed, cleaned and chopped
1 teaspoon freshly ground nutmeg + a dash more for garnish
1 cup diced celery
2 cooking apples such Courtland or Macintosh, cut into large chunks (approximately 2") with skin, then grated
1 cup unsweetened apple cider
6 cups low-sodium chicken or vegetable stock
Freshly ground pepper
Fresh chives

> **Tony's Tip!**
>
> You can prepare the squash up to 2 days before preparing this soup.
>
> Adding roasted garlic will rock this dish.

Directions:
Preheat oven to 375°F.
Cut bottom of squash so you have a flat surface. Cut squash in half lengthwise. Scoop out seeds with spoon and remove any stringy bits. Place squash cut side down on tinfoil-lined roasting dish.
Roast squash for 45–60 minutes or until squash becomes soft to touch.
Turn off oven. Let sit for up to 4 hours. You may wish to leave in oven and keep oven door partially open to cool quicker.
Once squash is cool to the touch, scoop out flesh and remove skin. Place into bowl.
Warm oil in large sauce or soup pot over medium heat.
Add leeks and stir. Cook for 3–4 minutes.
Add squash pulp, nutmeg, celery and grated apple and stir.
Cook for 2–4 minutes.
Add cider and stock, increase heat and cover.
Bring to a slow boil. Simmer uncovered for 30–40 minutes or desired texture.
Blend with immersion blender.
Garnish with freshly ground nutmeg and chives.

Variant: Stir in frozen spinach just before serving for a funky green, savory variation.

Roasted Sweet Potato Soup

Serves 4

Ingredients:

2 medium or large sweet potatoes, washed
1 tablespoon olive oil
2 leeks, trimmed, cleaned and chopped
2–3 medium carrots, chopped
1 cup diced celery
1 garlic clove, finely minced
1 teaspoon cayenne pepper (optional)
½ teaspoon salt
Freshly ground pepper
3–4 cups low-sodium chicken or vegetable stock
1 apple, grated and soaked in lemon juice
Fresh nutmeg to taste

> ### Tony's Tip!
>
> Substitute cinnamon or pumpkin spice blend in place of nutmeg.
>
> This can be prepared in advance.

Directions:

Preheat oven to 400°F.

Wrap sweet potatoes in tinfoil and bake in oven for 40–50 minutes until potatoes are soft. Once cooled, remove potatoes' flesh and set aside.

Warm oil in large sauce or soup pot over medium heat.

Add leeks and salt. Sauté until leeks are soft, 3–5 minutes.

Stir in carrots, celery and garlic. Cook for 2–3 minutes.

Add cayenne pepper, salt and pepper, stir. Cook 1–2 minutes.

Add sweet potato purée and stir. Cook 1–2 minutes.

Pour in stock and cover. Increase heat to medium high and bring to a slow boil.

Simmer uncovered for 15–20 minutes or until vegetables are cooked.

Blend with immersion blender if desired.

Mix in grated apple and dust with fresh nutmeg.

Gazpacho with Dill

Serves 4–6

Ingredients:

1 can (about 14 ounces) low-sodium diced tomatoes

½–¾ cup tomato or vegetable juice

1 cup diced cucumber

1 medium red onion, diced

1 green pepper, diced

1–2 jalapeño pepper, diced

½–1 cup radishes, washed and halved

Juice of 3–4 limes

3 tablespoons red wine vinegar

1 tablespoon horseradish

1–2 tablespoons extra virgin olive oil

½ cup fresh dill

Lots of fresh black pepper

Directions:

Combine ingredients in two batches in a blender.

Purée until smooth.

Place purée in large bowl and mix.

Chill for 2–8 hours.

Toast whole grain pita until crispy and serve with chilled gazpacho.

> Tony's Tip!
>
> For a crazy refreshing twist, consider adding some chopped, seedless watermelon to this.

Mains

Dinner is another one of those meals that falls by the wayside as the day creeps along. Before you know it, it's take-out again or other processed crap. Take a litle time during the week to plan your meals (and enlist the family to help with food prep). Many of these meals freeze well, and you can keep cooked brown rice, barley and cut vegetables in the refrigerator for days. With some simple meal planning, you can have meals that are as simple as "heat and eat" when you get home.

Rubs

Southern Twist:

Ideal for poultry, lamb or beef
1–2 tablespoons sweet or hot paprika (Hungarian paprika works well too)
1–2 teaspoons ground ginger
1–2 teaspoons cayenne pepper
1–2 teaspoons mustard powder
1 teaspoon cinnamon or ground cloves or nutmeg
1 teaspoon pepper
¼ teaspoon salt (optional)

Mediterranean:

Ideal for pork, poultry, white fish fillets or veggies
1 tablespoon oregano
1 tablespoon fresh thyme or dried basil
1 tablespoon lemon or lime zest (finely minced or grated)
1–2 garlic cloves, finely chopped or 1 teaspoon garlic powder
1 teaspoon pepper
¼ teaspoon salt (optional)

Moroccan:

Ideal for poultry, lamb or beef
1–2 tablespoons paprika
1–2 teaspoons ground ginger
1 teaspoon cinnamon
1 teaspoon ground cloves or ground nutmeg
1 teaspoon pepper
¼ teaspoon salt (optional)

Greek Pickle:

Ideal for poultry, pork, shrimp, white fish fillets or veggies
1 tablespoon oregano
2–3 tablespoons fresh dill
1 tablespoon ground coriander
1 teaspoon ground fennel seed
1 teaspoon pepper
¼ teaspoon salt (optional)

Indian Spice:

Ideal for poultry, pork or tofu
1–2 tablespoons curry powder
1–2 tablespoons chili flakes
1 tablespoon ground cumin
1 teaspoon turmeric
1 teaspoon dried mint
1 teaspoon pepper
1 teaspoon salt (optional)

Crazy Cajun:

Ideal for poultry, pork, salmon, white fish fillets or veggies
1–2 tablespoons cayenne pepper
1–2 tablespoons chili flakes
1 tablespoon garlic powder
1 teaspoon mustard powder
1 teaspoon oregano or basil
1 teaspoon pepper
1 teaspoon salt (optional)
½ teaspoon celery salt (optional)

Quick & Easy Marinades

Zesty Citrus:

Ideal for poultry, pork or fish fillets
½ cup lime or lemon juice
1 tablespoons chili oil
1–2 jalapeño peppers, sliced with or without seeds
4–6 green onions, sliced
Zest of 1–2 limes or 1 lemon
1–2 tablespoons fresh oregano or thyme
1 teaspoon pepper
½ teaspoon salt (optional)

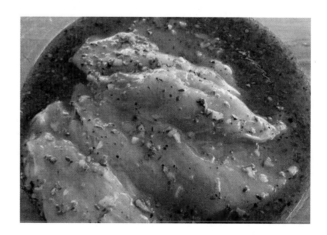

Mains

Asian Twist:

Ideal for poultry, pork, salmon or white fish fillets

½ cup low-sodium chicken stock

1 tablespoon sesame oil

1 tablespoon chili flakes

¼–½ cup fresh orange juice

Zest of one orange

1 tablespoon fresh grated ginger

2–4 garlic cloves, finely minced

2 teaspoons mustard powder (optional)

Creamy Curry:

Ideal for poultry, pork, salmon or white fish fillets

1 cup unflavored Greek yogurt

4 shallots, finely chopped

1–2 tablespoons curry powder

1 tablespoon fresh black pepper

1 teaspoon turmeric

1 teaspoon cumin

1 tablespoon fresh ginger, grated

2–4 garlic gloves, finely minced

Creamy Mustard:

Ideal for poultry, pork, salmon or white fish fillets

1 cup unflavored Greek yogurt

4 tablespoon Dijon or grainy mustard

1 tablespoon hot sauce (optional)

1 teaspoon mustard powder

Soy & Citrus Marinade:

1 lemon or lime (juice and zest)

½ cup low-sodium chicken stock

1 tablespoon low-sodium soy

2 garlic cloves, chopped (optional)

1 teaspoon pepper

> **Tony's Tip!**
>
> Combine ingredients in Zip-loc bag or Tupperware container so that chicken is well coated. Marinate at least two hours for chicken and no more than two hours for fish. Cook until through and juices run clear.

102

Peanut Chicken Curry with Veggies

Serves 4

Ingredients:

2 tablespoons olive oil, divided

4 boneless skinless chicken breasts, cut into 1" cubes

1 medium onion, quartered

2–3 medium carrots, sliced about ¼"

1–2 cloves garlic, minced

1 tablespoon curry powder

1 teaspoon turmeric

1 teaspoon chili flakes

Pinch of salt and fresh black pepper

2 tablespoons crunchy peanut butter

1 cup green beans, halved

1 can (15 ounces) diced tomatoes

1–2 cups broccoli florets

¼ cup coarsely chopped unsalted peanuts for garnish

Freshly chopped parsley or cilantro for garnish

Cooked brown rice (page 128) or soba noodles cooked according to directions on packaging

Directions:

Heat 1 tablespoon of olive oil in large skillet or Dutch oven. Add chicken pieces and toss until almost cooked through.

Remove with slotted spoon and set chicken aside.

Add remaining 1 tablespoon olive oil. Sauté onions and carrots until onions soften slightly.

Add garlic, curry powder, turmeric, chili flakes, salt and pepper. Coat onions and carrots with spices.

Add peanut butter and stir.

Mix in tomatoes, green beans and broccoli.

Add browned chicken.

Cook for 2–4 minutes until chicken is cooked through.

Turn off heat. Allow to sit for 5–10 minutes.

Serve on brown rice or soba noodles.

Garnish with chopped peanuts and parsley or cilantro.

Tony's Tip!

Substitute cauliflower in place of broccoli.

Grilled Cayenne Chicken on Brown Rice with Steamed Potatoes & Vegetables

Serves 4

Ingredients:

4 boneless skinless chicken breasts

2 lemons, juice and zest

½ cup stock (enough to immerse chicken in liquid)

1 teaspoon dried oregano or 2 teaspoons fresh (optional)

1 teaspoon cayenne pepper or more as desired

1–2 garlic cloves, finely chopped

Salt and fresh black pepper to taste

4 medium new potatoes, cleaned and quartered

½ red onion, thinly sliced

1 teaspoon cayenne pepper as desired

Fresh black pepper to taste

2 cups cooked brown rice (page 128)

Directions:

Combine first seven ingredients in Ziploc bag or in covered glass container. Allow to sit for at least two hours or up to overnight.

Steam or boil potatoes. Cook until fork tender, about 20 minutes.

Meanwhile, grill chicken for 7–9 minutes per side or roast in oven at 350–375°F for approximately 20–25 minutes until internal temperature reaches 175–180°F at its thickest point. You may need to oil grill to prevent sticking.

Allow cooked chicken to rest for 5–10 minutes.

Add sliced onions and spices to potatoes while they are still hot.

Serve side vegetables as desired.

Tony's Tip!

With time you will be able to gauge if chicken is cooked by poking it with your finger. If rock-hard it's overdone. Too soft means not cooked.

Grilled Lemon Rosemary Chicken with Whole Wheat Penne, Sweet Potatoes and Vegetables

Serves 4

Ingredients:

4 boneless skinless chicken breasts

1–2 lemons, juice and zest

½ cup low-sodium chicken stock

1 tablespoon low-sodium soy

2–4 sprigs fresh rosemary or 2–3 teaspoons dried rosemary

1–2 garlic cloves, chopped

1 teaspoon pepper

3–4 cups whole wheat penne pasta, cooked as per package instructions (reserve ¼ cup of pasta water)

1 tablespoon low-sodium soy sauce

Black pepper

Desired vegetables such as diced red pepper, chopped string beans or radish

Directions:

Combine first seven ingredients in Ziploc bag or in covered glass container. Allow to sit for at least two hours or up to overnight.

Grill chicken for 8–12 minutes per side or roast in oven at 350–375°F for approximately 20–25 minutes until internal temperature reaches 175–180°F at its thickest point. You may need to oil grill to prevent sticking. Allow cooked chicken to rest for 5–10 minutes.

Serve over pasta with cooked vegetables on side.

> **Tony's Tip!**
>
> Substitute kamut or spelt pasta for added nutrients and flavor.

Baked Cayenne-Mustard Chicken and Barley & Black Rice Blend with Vegetables

Serves 4
Ingredients:
4 boneless skinless chicken breasts
4 tablespoons Dijon mustard
1 tablespoon low-sodium soy sauce
1–2 garlic cloves, chopped
1 teaspoon cayenne pepper
Cooked Barley & Black Rice Blend (page 131)
Cooked vegetables of your choice

Directions:
Combine first five ingredients in Ziploc bag or in covered glass container. Allow to sit for at least two hours or up to overnight.
Grill chicken for 7–10 minutes per side or roast in oven 350–375°F for approximately 20–25 minutes until internal temperature reaches 175–180°F at its thickest point. You may need to oil grill to prevent sticking.
Allow cooked chicken to rest for 5–10 minutes.
Serve over rice with cooked vegetables on side.

Tony's Tip!

Substitute brown and wild rice (page 128) to keep things interesting.

Grilled Chicken with Zesty Mango Mustard Purée, Grilled Vegetables and Steamed Snap Peas

Serves 4

Ingredients:

4 boneless skinless chicken breasts

¼ cup apple cider vinegar or rice wine vinegar

½ cup chicken stock or more if needed

1–2 tablespoons Dijon or grainy mustard

3 garlic cloves, coarsely chopped

½ teaspoon mustard powder

1 teaspoon pepper to taste

Selection of peppers, red onions and zucchini, sliced

Directions:

Combine first seven ingredients in Ziploc bag or in covered glass container. Allow to sit for at least two hours or up to overnight. In a separate bag or container, combine all vegetables and marinate for at least an hour or up to overnight.

Grill chicken for 8–12 minutes per side or roast in oven at 350–375°F for approximately 20–25 minutes until internal temperature reaches 175–180°F at its thickest point. You may need to oil grill to prevent sticking. Allow cooked chicken to rest for 5–10 minutes.

Grill vegetables until desired texture, approximately 1–2 minutes per side or use wire grill baskets.

Grilled Chicken on a Rice Medley with Vegetables with a Tomato Sauce

Serves 4

Ingredients:

4 boneless skinless chicken breasts, marinated according to directions in previous recipes (see page 112 for marinade suggestions)

Vegetables of choice, for side

Cooked rice (page 128)

½ cup tomato purée or strained tomatoes

½ cup low-sodium chicken stock

1 garlic clove, finely minced

Fresh black pepper to taste

Directions:

Mix all ingredients for tomato sauce in small saucepan. Heat until warm to the touch (do not boil).

Simmer for 3–5 minutes.

Plate and enjoy!

Chicken Curry Stir Fry

Serves 4

Ingredients:

2–3 tablespoons canola oil or olive oil, divided

2 teaspoons sesame oil, divided

4 boneless chicken breasts cut into 2" strips

8–10 button mushrooms, cleaned and chopped into quarters

1–2 garlic cloves, finely chopped

Pinch of salt and fresh black pepper to taste

1 large onion, sliced

¼–½ cup low-sodium chicken stock

1 tablespoon red curry paste

Carrots as desired, finely sliced

Combination of large green, red or orange peppers, sliced

6–8 Roma tomatoes, chopped or 1 can (14 ounces) diced Roma tomatoes

3–4 leaves fresh basil, torn

Directions:

Heat 1 tablespoon of canola oil and sesame oil in a wok or large sauté pan over medium high heat.

Add chicken, cook for 6–8 minutes until chicken is fully cooked.

Remove chicken and set aside.

Add 1 tablespoon of canola oil.

Add mushrooms and cook until they become caramelized.

Remove mushrooms and set aside in bowl. Toss with garlic, salt and fresh black pepper.

Add final tablespoon of canola oil and sesame oil.

Add onions and sauté for approximately 2–3 minutes. Add ¼ cup stock.

Add curry paste and carrots. Toss for 3–5 minutes.

Add peppers, sauté for 2–3 minutes. Add more stock, if necessary.

Add chopped tomatoes with any liquid from tomatoes.

Add cooked chicken and mushrooms.

Combine well, stir for 2–4 minutes.

Add basil and fresh pepper when done.

Serve on brown rice.

> **Tony's Tip!**
>
> Select curry paste without added sugar. Many will have sugar as first ingredients.

Grilled Turkey Cutlet with Whole Wheat Penne and Veggies

Serves 4

Ingredients:

4 tablespoons paprika, such as Hungarian or smoked

1 tablespoon cayenne pepper

1 tablespoon garlic powder

1 teaspoon onion powder

½ teaspoon salt

4 turkey cutlets, approximately 6 ounces pounded flat to about ¾" thick

2 cups uncooked whole wheat penne

1 tablespoon low-sodium soy sauce

Fresh black pepper to taste

Vegetables such as diced red pepper and broccoli for side

Tony's Tip!

Works as well with chicken or lean pork cutlets.

Directions:

Thoroughly mix paprika, cayenne pepper, garlic powder, onion powder and salt in bowl.

Spread spice mix evenly on flat dish. Dredge cutlets in spice mix or put cutlets and spices in Ziploc bag, seal and shake bag vigorously until cutlets are well coated. Shake off excess.

Grill cutlets at medium high heat for 4–6 minutes per side, depending on thickness of cutlet.

Meanwhile, cook pasta according to package instructions. Drain pasta, reserving about ¼ cup of cooking water. Toss pasta with water, soy sauce and black pepper to create a sauce.

Moroccan Greek Chicken & Grilled Veggies

Serves 4

Ingredients:

½ cup unflavored Greek yogurt

4 tablespoons lemon juice, divided

1–3 garlic cloves, crushed + 1 clove, finely chopped

4 teaspoons grated fresh ginger, divided

2 tablespoons fresh dill

½–1 teaspoon ground cinnamon

½–1 teaspoon ground cloves

½–1 teaspoon coriander

Pinch of salt and fresh black pepper

4 boneless skinless chicken breasts

Vegetables such as red onions, peppers, zucchini and portobello mushrooms, chopped

2 tablespoons olive oil

2 tablespoons balsamic vinegar

> **Tony's Tip!**
>
> If necessary, substitute one third the amount of dried herbs for fresh herbs in this recipe.

Directions:

Combine yogurt, 2 tablespoons lemon juice, spices and herbs in glass or Pyrex dish. Add chicken, making sure that chicken is well coated. Cover and allow to marinate 2–24 hours.

Whisk remaining lemon juice, olive oil, balsamic vinegar, garlic and ginger in large bowl. Toss in vegetables until well coated. Allow to sit for 1–2 hours if possible.

Grill chicken, about 6–8 minutes per side. Allow to sit for at least 3–5 minutes before slicing.

Grill vegetables until cooked to desired tenderness.

Place grilled vegetables on platter and serve with sliced chicken on top.

Serve with brown rice, quinoa or whole wheat couscous.

Garnish with fresh cilantro.

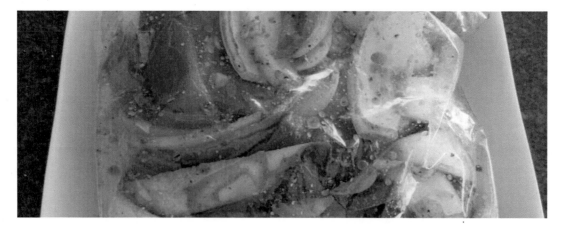

Chicken Veggie Puttanesca

Serves 4
Ingredients:
2 tablespoons olive oil
4 boneless skinless chicken breasts evenly flattened to ¾" thick
¼ cup fresh parsley or basil, chopped, plus more for garnish
1 teaspoon chili flakes, divided
2 medium onions, quartered
4 garlic cloves, finely chopped
Pinch of salt and fresh black pepper
2 cans (15 ounces) of tomatoes, strained
1 cup frozen spinach or kale (optional)
2–3 cups button mushroom, cleaned and cut into quarters
1 teaspoon dried oregano
¼ cup capers or sliced olives (optional)
Whole wheat pasta, cooked according to directions on packaging

Directions:
Preheat oven to 375°F.
Heat oil over medium heat in a Dutch oven.
Sear chicken for 3–4 minutes per side. Chicken will not be cooked through.
Remove partially cooked chicken and set aside. Sprinkle chicken with fresh basil and half of chili flakes.
Sauté onions with a clean utensil for 2–3 minutes.
Add garlic, remaining chili flakes, salt and pepper. Continue to mix for 2–3 minutes until onions are soft.
Add tomatoes. Cover and cook on medium high heat until mixture bubbles.
Reduce to medium low heat, and add frozen spinach. Add mushrooms and simmer uncovered, stirring occasionally, for 15 minutes to thicken mixture.
Add chicken to mixture. Be sure to submerge chicken.
Cover dish and bake in oven for 20–30 minutes.
Turn off oven and allow to rest. Close to serving time, cook pasta if not already done and serve with side vegetables such as asparagus.
Plate together and garnish with more fresh basil, oregano and capers or sliced olives.

Chicken Marinades

Yogurt Citrus Marinade:

Juice of 2 lemons + zest of 1
1 cup unflavored Greek yogurt
1–2 teaspoon of desired fresh or dried herbs such as rosemary, thyme, oregano, basil

Directions:
Whisk all ingredients and place with chicken in a Ziploc bag or Pyrex container. Marinate for 4 hours or overnight.
Variant: Substitute chopped Turkish apricots for herbs for an apricot infusion to this marinade.

Tandoori Masala Marinade:

Juice of 2 lemons or 3 limes + zest of 1
1 cup unflavored Greek yogurt
2 teaspoons Tandoori masala

Directions:
Whisk all ingredients and place with chicken in a Ziploc bag or in Pyrex container. Marinate for 4 hours or overnight.

Soy & Citrus Marinade:

1–2 lemons or 3–4 limes, juice and zest
2 garlic cloves, chopped
½ cup low-sodium chicken stock
1 tablespoon low-sodium soy sauce
1 teaspoon black pepper
Lemongrass (optional)
Dried lime leaves (optional)

> **Tony's Tip!**
>
> Discard yogurt marinades once used and do not consume.
>
> You can freeze chicken with their marinade for convenience.

> **Tony's Tip!**
>
> Lemongrass can be used in marinades, stir-fries, or soups. When using, be sure to remove before serving – you can choke on it.

Simple Turkey Burger Patties

Serves 4
Ingredients:
1 pound ground turkey breast
¼ cup dried whole wheat bread crumbs or Scottish oats
1 small onion chopped or 2 medium shallots
1–2 tablespoons parsley or use sage, finely chopped
1–2 eggs
Splash of Worcestershire or Tabasco sauce
Pinch of salt
4 whole wheat buns
Veggies for burgers such as lettuce, tomatoes, cucumbers and red onion

Directions:
Combine first six ingredients in a bowl. Add additional egg if too dry.
Form into four evenly shaped patties.
Cover and let stand until ready to grill.
Cook burger patties until well done about 4–5 minutes a side.
Assemble and enjoy.

Lean Pork Loin with Tomato Rice & Veggies

Serves 2
Ingredients:
1 teaspoon mustard powder (or use any rub on page 100–101)
2 pork loin chops, any visible fat removed
Cooked rice (page 128) with chopped Roma tomatoes
Steamed vegetables of choice

Directions:
Rub spice mixture onto meat.
Grill pork 3–5 minutes per side.
Serve with rice, tomatoes and steamed vegetables.

Cranberry Turkey Burger Patties

Serves 4

Ingredients:

1 pound ground turkey breast

1 egg

2 small shallots, finely chopped

½ cup unflavored instant oats

¼ cup fresh cranberries, chopped

1–2 tablespoons low-sodium rice wine vinegar

1 tablespoon grainy Dijon mustard

1 tablespoon sage, finely chopped

Salt and fresh black pepper

4 whole wheat buns

Veggies for burgers such as lettuce, tomatoes, cucumbers and red onion

Asian Slaw on page 56 (optional)

Directions:

Combine first nine ingredients in large bowl. Add more vinegar or oats to thin or thicken to desired texture.

Form into four evenly shaped patties.

Cover and let stand until ready to grill.

Cook burger patties until well done about 4–6 minutes a side.

Assemble and enjoy.

> ### Tony's Tip!
>
> Always select extra-lean ground meat rather than lean. It has less fat.

Easy Turkey Meatloaf with Snuck-in Vegetables

Serves 4

Ingredients:

2 ribs of celery to be used as a base for the meat loaf

1 pound extra-lean ground turkey

2 ribs of celery, finely chopped or 1 zucchini, grated

1–2 large carrots, grated

1 large onion, grated

2 eggs

¾ cup instant unflavored oats (more if needed)

2 tablespoons grainy or Dijon mustard

1 tablespoon sage, finely chopped

1–2 teaspoons orange rind, finely chopped

Fresh black pepper

Pinch of salt

> Tony's Tip!
>
> This makes for great leftovers.

Directions:

Preheat oven to 350°F.

Spray a large nonstick loaf pan with cooking spray. Place ribs of celery on the bottom of loaf pan to allow for any excess fat to drip to base. You can also use carrots or mesh tray.

Mix remaining ingredients together in large bowl.

Form into a loaf and place it in loaf pan.

Bake for about 40–50 minutes.

About 30 minutes into cooking, insert knife to check for doneness. The knife will come out clean when loaf is cooked through.

Once fully cooked, turn off oven and let rest for 15–20 minutes.

Serve with Cranberry Chutney (page 69) and boiled potatoes.

Grilled Trout on a Rice Medley with Steamed Veggies

Serves 4

Ingredients:

6 new potatoes, washed and quartered

Vegetables such as carrots, green beans and asparagus

4 trout or salmon fillets

Lemon wedges

Fresh black pepper to taste

Finely sliced red onion to taste

Cayenne pepper to taste

> **Tony's Tip!**
>
> Frozen fish is a great and easy alternative to fresh fish when not available. Always have some in your freezer.

Directions:

Steam or boil potatoes until fork tender, about 20 minutes.

Steam or boil vegetables until desired texture.

Lightly oil grill. Cook fish non-skin side first (primarily for presentation but it helps the fish stay in one piece), approximately 6–7 minutes per side.

Squeeze fresh lemon on fish while warm.

Add finely sliced red onions and cayenne pepper to potatoes.

Steamed Salmon with Soy & Orange Juice on Brown Basmati Rice

Serves 2

Ingredients:

2 salmon fillets

2 tablespoons freshly squeezed orange juice

2 teaspoons low-sodium soy sauce

1–2 teaspoons finely minced garlic

Lemon wedges

Almond slivers for garnish

1 cup cooked brown rice or rice medley (page 128)

Cooked vegetables such as string beans, broccoli or cauliflower

Directions:

Steam salmon fillets in steamer, skin side down, approximately 12–15 minutes or until salmon are just cooked through. Do not overcook!

Mix orange juice, soy sauce and garlic in small bowl. Drizzle sauce onto salmon, garnish with lemon and almonds.

Serve with rice and vegetables.

Tony's Tip!

This dressing works well with white fish too.

117

Steamed Salmon on a Bed of Rice Medley, Side Vegetables & Yogurt Scallion Sauce

Serves 4

Ingredients:

4 salmon fillets

3 tablespoons Greek yogurt or plain, unflavored yogurt

½ garlic clove, finely chopped (optional)

Lemon juice to taste

2–3 green onions, sliced or fresh dill

¾ cup cooked white and wild rice (page 128)

Lemon wedges for garnish

> **Tony's Tip!**
>
> In my early days of weight loss, eating brown rice was tough so I mixed white and brown or white and wild rice.

Directions:

Steam salmon fillets in steamer skin side down, approximately 15 minutes or until salmon are just cooked though. Do not overcook!

Mix yogurt, garlic and lemon juice. Add green onions or dill.

Place cooked salmon over rice and drizzle sauce over all. Enjoy!

Baked Red Snapper Fillet on Citrus Couscous Topped with Tapenade

Serves 4

Ingredients:

1½ cups uncooked couscous

Cinnamon stick or star anise (optional)

3 cups boiling water

Freshly squeezed lemon juice to taste

8–10 green olives, coarsely chopped

2–3 Roma tomatoes, diced

Jalapeño pepper to taste, finely chopped

1 tablespoon capers (can be found in ethnic section of supermarket)

1 tablespoon olive oil

4 red snapper fillets or other white fish fillets

Green beans, diced red peppers and walnuts (optional)

Directions:

Place couscous and cinnamon stick or star anise in a heatproof bowl. Add boiling water, cover bowl with lid, and allow couscous to sit for 45–60 minutes until couscous has doubled in size. Remove cinnamon stick or star anise. Fluff with fork. Add freshly squeezed lemon juice. This holds well in fridge for days.

Mix olives, tomatoes, jalapeño peppers, capers, olive oil and more lemon juice in small bowl. Set aside.

Preheat oven to 400°F. Bake snapper fillets on tinfoil-lined baking dish for 7–10 minutes or until done. You may need to turn fish over once depending on thickness.

Serve fish on bed of couscous, topped with tapenade. Garnish with green beans, diced red peppers and walnuts. Enjoy!

> *Tony's Tip!*
>
> Add a cinnamon stick, star anise or saffron with couscous for African flare.

Salmon Burger with Diluted Mayo
& Roasted Sweet Potato Fries

Serves 4

Ingredients:

1 tablespoon low-fat mayonnaise

1 tablespoon lemon juice

Sliced green onions or fresh dill (optional)

2 large sweet potatoes

1–2 teaspoons olive oil

1–2 teaspoons cinnamon or cayenne pepper or combination of spices

¼ teaspoon salt

Whole wheat thin burger buns

4 salmon burgers (President's Choice Blue Menu or Compliments brand can be found in frozen fish section or see opposite page for homemade recipe)

Veggies for burgers such as lettuce, tomatoes and red onion

Directions:

Combine mayonnaise, lemon juice and green onions or dill in small bowl. Set aside.

Cut sweet potatoes into large matchsticks. Toss with oil, cinnamon and salt.

Roast fries at 450°F on tinfoil-lined baking sheet for approximately 6–7 minutes, flip once and continue roasting for another 6–7 minutes.

Grill burgers as per package instructions. Plate and enjoy!

> **Tony's Tip!**
>
> When purchasing meat patties or frozen chicken always review ingredients to make sure you are buying meat and not fillers. Avoid starches and crazy chemicals added to meat.

Homemade Salmon Burger Patties

Serves 4
Ingredients:
1 pound salmon fillets, cut into cubes with skin removed
¼ cup dried whole wheat bread crumbs or Scottish oats
1 teaspoon grated fresh ginger
1 large shallot, finely chopped
1 tablespoon fresh dill or 1 teaspoon dried dill
1–2 eggs
Pinch of salt
4 whole wheat buns
Veggies for burgers such as lettuce, tomatoes, cucumbers and red onion

Directions:
Combine salmon, bread crumbs, ginger, shallots, dill, eggs and salt in food processor.
Process until well combined. Add additional eggs if needed.
Form into four evenly shaped patties.
Cover and let stand until ready to grill.
Cook burger patties on medium high heat until well done about 3–4 minutes a side.
Assemble and enjoy.

Broiled Asian Citrus Salmon on Rice Medley with Steamed Vegetables

Serves 4

Ingredients:

Juice of 2 lemons or more as desired

2 tablespoons low-sodium soy sauce

2–3 garlic cloves, chopped

1 tablespoon chopped fresh ginger (optional but a good idea)

2–3 shallots, sliced or finely sliced sweet onions

Fresh black pepper or peppercorns to taste

4 salmon fillets

Lemon wedges

Cooked rice medley (page 128)

Desired vegetables

Directions:

Combine first six ingredients for salmon marinade.

Place salmon and marinade in Ziploc bag or glass or Pyrex dish. Allow to sit for up to 2 hours.

Preheat oven to broil low.

Place fish on tinfoil-lined baking dish.

Pour marinade over fish, placing shallot slices on top of salmon so they will crisp.

Broil on low for 10–12 minutes. Prepare side vegetables while fish cooks.

Increase to high broil for another 2–4 minutes. Continue to monitor to avoid burning. The shallots or onions should caramelize a little.

Remove from oven. Squeeze with fresh lemon.

Serve with cooked rice and vegetables. Enjoy!

Tony's Tip!

Marinating fish for longer than 2 hours with lemon juice will actually begin to cook fish.

Shrimp with Rice Medley, Grilled Peppers & Steamed Vegetables

Serves 4
Ingredients:
3 large orange or red peppers
¼ cup red wine vinegar
1 tablespoon balsamic vinegar
1 garlic clove, finely chopped
Mrs. Dash seasoning or dried herbs such as oregano or rosemary
Salt and fresh black pepper to taste
20 ounces medium shrimp, shelled and deveined
3 whole garlic cloves
Fresh black pepper to taste
Lemon wedges

> **Tony's Tip!**
>
> When selecting dried herb mixture be sure to review ingredients. Many will have sugar or salt as the primary ingredients.

Directions:
Combine first six ingredients and allow to marinate for 1 hour or overnight.
Boil or grill shrimp just until they turn pink and curl. Do not overcook. Drain and toss with garlic, pepper and lemon or other spices like Mrs. Dash.
Serve immediately with steamed vegetables on the side.

Mains

Broiled Cayenne-Crusted Tilapia Fillets Served with Roasted Lemons & Onions

Serves 4
Ingredients:
2–3 tablespoons fine or medium corn meal
1 tablespoon cayenne pepper
¼ teaspoon salt
2 lemons, sliced about ¼" thick
2 cooking onions sliced about ¼" thick
2 white fish fillets such as tilapia, basa, etc., pat dry
with paper towel to remove any extra moisture

Directions:
Preheat oven on low broil or 425°F.
Combine flour, cayenne pepper and salt in
small bowl and set aside.
Arrange sliced lemons and onions on tinfoil-
lined baking sheet.
Place fish on top of lemon/onion slices.
Evenly sprinkle flour mixture on top of fish.
Place baking sheet on upper shelf of oven.
Cook for 5–8 minutes or until fish flakes eas-
ily with a fork. To get a "fried" crust, broil on
high heat for 30–90 seconds.
Serve with roasted and steamed vegetables.
Garnish with cooked onions and lemons.
Roasting lemons cuts their acidity so you can
eat them.

Tony's Tip!

This technique can be used
with any white fish fillets
like basa, cod, red snapper,
etc.

124

Seared Salmon on Bed of Brown Rice with Lots of Veggies

Serves 2
Ingredients:
2 salmon fillets
1 tablespoon canola oil
Juice of 1 lemon
1–2 garlic cloves, finely minced or 1 teaspoon from jar
Cooked brown rice (page 128)
Steamed vegetables of choice

> **Tony's Tip!**
>
> To save time, broil salmon with any spice blend such as Mrs. Dash.

Directions:
Preheat oven to 400°F.
Pat salmon fillets dry with paper towel to remove excess moisture.
Heat oil in heavy non-stick pan over medium high heat. Place salmon fillet skin side up. Sear about 2 minutes.
Remove fish from pan, place salmon in baking dish.
Cook for 12–15 minutes or until dark pink all the way through. Remove from oven.
Squeeze lemon juice onto fish and brush with garlic.
Serve fish on brown rice and vegetables.

Grilled Marlin on Rice with Fresh Tomato Jalapeño Salsa & Veggies

Serves 2
Ingredients:
2 sushi-grade marlin or tuna steaks, about 2" thick
¼ teaspoon sea salt

Tomato Jalapeño Salsa

Makes 1 cup
Ingredients:
4 Roma tomatoes, skins removed, chopped
1–2 tablespoons olive oil
1 small shallot, finely minced or ½ red onion, finely minced
1 jalapeño pepper, finely chopped and seeded
¼ cup red wine vinegar, balsamic vinegar or combination
4–5 basil leaves, torn
Salt and pepper as desired

Directions:
Preheat grill on high. Lightly season fish on both sides with sea salt.
Grill 2–3 minutes per side.
Combine remaining ingredients in bowl.
Serve on fish.

> **Tony's Tip!**
>
> With sushi-grade seafood there is no need to cook fish through. The rarer (ie. undercooked) the better.

Vegetable & Bean Curry

Serves 2

Ingredients:

2 tablespoons canola oil

1 teaspoon sesame oil

2 teaspoons fresh ginger, finely minced

1 large Spanish onion, cut in large chunks

1 tablespoon curry powder of choice

2 teaspoons turmeric

¼ teaspoon salt

Fresh black pepper to taste

1 green pepper, chopped

1 jalapeño pepper, finely chopped

1 cup carrots, cut into large chunks

¾–1 cup celery, sliced

1 can (28 ounces) of diced tomatoes

1 cup broccoli florets

1 cup green beans, cut in half

1 can (28 ounces) of kidney beans, rinsed and drained

¾ cup corn

1 cup cooked brown rice (page 128)

Juice of 1–2 limes

Tony's Tip!

Use spelt, kamut, soba or whole wheat pasta to mix things up.

Directions:

Heat oils on low to medium heat in large sauté pan or wok.

Add ginger, cook, stirring, for 1–2 minutes.

Increase heat to medium high.

Add onions, curry powder, turmeric, salt and black pepper and cook, stirring, until onions slightly soften, about 2–4 minutes.

Add green peppers, jalapeño peppers, carrots and celery, stir. Cook for 3–4 minutes.

Add tomatoes with liquid, broccoli, and green beans.

Add beans and mix well.

Add corn and continue to cook for 2–3 minutes.

Add lime juice.

Serve on rice.

Easy Peasy Brown Rice

Serves 8
Ingredients:
4 cups water, low-sodium chicken stock or combination of water and stock
2 cups brown rice
1 teaspoon olive oil

Directions:
Combine all ingredients in heavy pot and cover.
Bring to a boil. Turn down heat and simmer on very low heat for 30–40 minutes, covered.
Turn off heat and let sit for 15–20 minutes.
Uncover and fluff with fork for perfect rice.
Serve or set aside, placing in Tupperware containers for later in the week.

Brown & Wild Rice Medley

Serves 8
Ingredients:
4 cups water, low-sodium chicken stock or combination of water and stock
1¼ cup brown rice
¾ cup wild rice
1 teaspoon olive oil
Spices or herbs such as dried oregano, thyme or rosemary (optional)
Tabasco sauce (optional)

Directions:
Combine water, rice, olive oil in heavy pot and cover. Add optional spices. Bring water to a boil.
Simmer on very low heat or turn off for 45 minutes. Keep covered.
Turn off heat and let sit until needed.
Fluff with fork for perfect rice.
Serve or set aside.

> ### Tony's Tip!
> If you're not a fan of brown rice, try a blend of white and brown or white and wild rice to help you transition over to the "dark" side.

Quinoa

This is a basic recipe for cooking quinoa. You can use it in place of rice. Quinoa can be used as a source of carbohydrates or used as a complete protein. It is gluten free. It is prepared quickly and easily. You can even have it for beakfast; substitute milk for stock or water. Or use combination of water and milk.

Ingredients:

1 cup quinoa

2 cups water or low-sodium stock

Directions:

Rinse quinoa thoroughly under cold water, using a fine mesh strainer.

Place quinoa and water or stock in a medium saucepan and bring to a boil.

Reduce to a simmer, cover and cook until all of the water is absorbed, about 15 minutes.

You will know that the quinoa is done when all the grains have turned from white to transparent, and the grain has slightly separated.

Quinoa Trio with Jalapeño and a Hint of Mint Salad

Serves 4

Ingredients:

¾ cup yellow quinoa

¼ cup red quinoa

¼ cup black quinoa

2 cups low-sodium chicken stock

Juice and some zest of one lemon

1–2 medium jalapeño peppers, finely diced

6–8 fresh mint leaves, finely chopped

¼ cup dried, unsweetened cranberries

1 tablespoon Parmesan cheese (optional)

Fresh black pepper

> ### Tony's Tip!
>
> Combine yellow, red and black quinoa for a tri-color quinoa. This also makes a great snack. While taking night school during my weight loss, I always had a container of this for my night school break.

Directions:

Rinse quinoa thoroughly under cold water using fine mesh strainer.

Place rinsed quinoa in heavy saucepan with stock and some of the lemon zest and cover.

Bring to a slow boil. Immediately turn heat to lowest setting and leave covered for 45 minutes. Add the lemon juice and let rest for up to two hours. Add remaining ingredients to cooked quinoa in a bowl. Enjoy warm or cold. Stores well for great leftovers.

Rainbow Veggie Quinoa Salad

Serves 3–4
Ingredients:
4–5 tablespoons red wine vinegar
2–3 tablespoons olive oil
¼ cup fresh dill
1 cup shredded carrot
1 cup shredded zucchini
1 cup thinly sliced red onion
2 cups sliced red, yellow and green pepper
1 cup diced cucumber
½ cup grated or sliced radish
2 cups cooked quinoa
½ cup light feta cheese

Directions:
Combine vinegar, olive oil and dill in a large bowl. Add vegetables and toss with vinaigrette. Add quinoa. Crumble feta cheese over top. Serve as a side dish or combine with greens.

> Tony's Tip!
>
> Experiment with other vegetable combinations.

Dijon-Dressed Rainbow Veggie Quinoa Salad

Serves 3–4
Ingredients:
2 tablespoons olive oil
4 tablespoons white wine vinegar
1–2 tablespoons Dijon mustard
½ garlic clove, finely minced
Fresh black pepper
2 cups cooked quinoa
1 medium red onion, diced
1 pint cherry tomatoes, halved
1 cup fresh corn kernels
1 cup fresh basil leaves or ½ cup fresh mint
½ cup diced peppers

Directions:
Whisk together first five ingredients in small bowl for dressing. Mix rest of ingredients in large bowl and pour dressing over. Toss to combine.

Cooked Barley & Red, Black or Wild Rice Blend

Serves 8
Ingredients:
2 cups any combination of barley or rice
2 cups chicken stock
2–3 tablespoons hot sauce
2 tablespoons olive oil or butter
2 teaspoons dried oregano or any dried herb of choice

Directions:
Rinse rice and barley blend.
Place barley and rice mixture into rice cooker with stock, hot sauce and herb(s).
Bring to boil.

Simmer for 30–45 minutes.
Remove heat, stir in oil or butter and oregano.
Store in airtight container until ready to use.

Couscous & Bulgurs

For couscous (whole wheat) and bulgur, prepare as per directions in package.
Bulgur is great for breakfast too. Substitute milk for water and you have another breakfast of champions.

Mains' Side Dishes

Simple Pasta with Tomatoes

Serves 2

Ingredients:

1½–2 cups cooked whole wheat pasta such as linguine, penne or rotini

1 can (about 14 ounces) low-sodium canned tomatoes

1 garlic clove, finely chopped

Directions:

Cook pasta as directed on package.

Heat tomatoes and garlic in small saucepan.

Pour sauce over pasta.

Super Veggie Whole Wheat Penne Pasta

Serves 2

Ingredients:

2 cups whole wheat pasta such as penne or fusilli

¼ cup red wine or balsamic vinegar

2 tablespoons hummus

1 tablespoon Parmesan cheese (optional)

1½ cups cooked broccoli florets or other vegetable such as string beans or asparagus spears

1 medium red onion, thinly sliced

4–5 radishes, sliced

2 pints cherry tomatoes, halved

1 cup grated carrots

6 basil sprigs, chopped

Leftover cooked chicken or use canned legumes of choice

> **Tony's Tip!**
>
> Cook pasta in same water that you cooked vegetables for additional flavor.

Directions:

Cook pasta as per directions on package. Drain, reserving ¼ cup of pasta water .

Toss warm cooked pasta with hummus and vinegar to create a "sauce."

Add Parmesan cheese.

Toss in vegetables and vinegar.

Add reserved pasta water if sauce looks too thick.

Garnish with basil.

Add desired protein or legumes.

Tasty Veggies Even Kids Will Eat!

This is where the traditional "calories in, calories out" model goes out the window as far as I and many others who prioritize eating whole foods for weight loss are concerned. It's not about eating less; it's about eating differently – the more vegetables the better. Most of us who struggle with weight are volume eaters and we need volume. So it has to be healthy volume and where better to get that than from veggies that are prepared healthfully?

Cauliflower Purée:

Makes about 2–3 cups
½ head of cauliflower, separated into florets (about 3 cups)
2 Vidalia onions, roasted or grilled (see next page)
½ cup unflavored Greek yogurt
1 tablespoon Parmesan or Romano cheese
1 teaspoon garlic purée
1 teaspoon dried oregano
Black pepper to taste

Directions:
Steam or boil cauliflower until starts to soften.
Place all ingredients in stand up blender. You may need to add a little liquid such as milk or stock to liquefy. Or place items in deep bowl and purée using a handheld blender.
Place purée in bowl and serve as a dip for vegetables or topping for whole grain crackers. No salt is needed if using grated cheese.

Caribbean Corn (No Butter Needed)

Ingredients:
1–2 teaspoons cayenne pepper
1–2 teaspoons paprika
1–2 teaspoons garlic powder
½–1 teaspoon ginger
¼ teaspoon salt (optional)
2 ears corn, washed and husked
Lemon or lime wedges

Directions:
Mix all spices and set side.
Boil corn in lightly salted water until kernels are soft when pricked with a fork, about 5 minutes at a heavy rolling boil.
Press lemon or lime wedges onto corn and dust the corn with spice mixture.

Boiled Beets:

Ingredients:
Beets

Directions:
Clean beets well. Do not peel.
Boil beets in covered pot for 15–20 minutes, reduce to medium heat.
Cook for another 30 minutes or until beets is soft.
Remove from water and allow to cool at room temperature. Once cool enough to handle, peel back skin and set beets aside. These keep in refrigerator for days or in mason jars with plain or flavored vinegar for weeks.

Roasted Parsnip & Onions:

Ingredients:
4 medium parsnips, cut into 2" chunks
Large Vidalia onions, cut into large chunks
1 teaspoon cayenne pepper
Salt and fresh black pepper to taste

Directions:
Preheat oven to 425°F.
Place all ingredients in baking dish and toss well to coat. Spread in even layer.
Roast in oven for 25–30 minutes.

Grilled Leeks

Ingredients:
Leeks, as many as desired
Olive oil
Salt to taste
Cayenne pepper (optional)
Herbs of choice

Directions:
Cut off top green section of leeks. Cut lengthwise, keeping root bottom on leek intact. Rinse leeks halves under cold water to remove any dirt that may be inside.
Lightly brush with olive oil, sprinkle some salt and desired seasonings such as cayenne or herbs on inner half of leeks. Grill on medium high grill for 3–4 minutes on each side, or until charred to desire.

Spinach Pesto

Makes about 2–3 cups
1 tablespoon olive oil
1 tablespoon butter
1–2 teaspoons sesame oil
4 cups button mushrooms, cleaned and quartered
2–3 garlic cloves, finely chopped
1 large onion, diced
1–2 teaspoons dried oregano
¼ cup low-sodium chicken stock
8–10 cups baby spinach
Fresh black pepper to taste

> Tony's Tip!
>
> This can be used as a pasta sauce or with rice.

Directions:
Heat oil and butter in large wok over medium to high heat. Brown mushrooms, about 5 minutes.
Add garlic, onions and oregano. Stir until onions are soft.
Add spinach in batches.
Once all spinach has wilted, season with pepper. Blend with immersion blender.
Use with rice or pasta. Keeps well in fridge.

Grilled Citrus Broccolini or Asparagus

Ingredients:
1 pound of or broccolini or asparagus stalks, woody stem removed
Lemon juice to taste
1 teaspoon Parmesan cheese (optional)

Directions:
Steam or boil asparagus for 1–2 minutes. Spritz or drizzle with lemon juice and grill on indoor or outdoor grill for 1–2 minutes or until slightly charred. Sprinkle with Parmesan cheese and enjoy. Asparagus spears make great leftovers.

Roasted Root Veggie Medley

Serves 4–6
3 tablespoons balsamic vinegar
1 tablespoon olive oil
2–3 medium carrots, cut into large chunks
2–3 celery stalks, cut into large pieces
2 medium parsnips, cut into large chunks
1 medium Vidalia onion, cut into quarters
6–8 garlics cloves, peeled
1 teaspoon fennel seeds or crushed mustard seeds
¼ teaspoon salt
Fresh black pepper or peppercorns to taste

Directions:
Preheat oven to 425°F.
Mix vinegar and oil and set aside.
Place carrots, celery, parsnips, onions and garlic into large tinfoil-lined baking dish.
Add fennel or mustard seeds, salt and pepper and toss well to coat.
Add oil-vinegar mixture and toss further.
Place into oven and roast for 50–60 minutes or until desired crispness.
Flip vegetables two or three times so they do not stick.

Tony's Tip!

This makes great leftovers. Beets or fennel work well with this dish too!

Roasted Tomatoes Infused with Garlic

Ingredients:
1 tablespoon olive oil
1 tablespoon garlic purée
1–2 teaspoon dried oregano or thyme
¼ teaspoon sea salt (optional)
Black pepper
12–15 ripe Roma tomatoes

Directions:
Preheat oven 425°F.
Combine oil, garlic and seasonings in small bowl. Set aside.
Cut Roma tomatoes in half lengthwise and place, cut side up, on large tinfoil-lined baking sheet.
Brush with oil mixture.
Bake on middle rack (or broil if you wish) until tomatoes slightly char about 10–12 minutes. Time will vary depending on oven. Reserve any tomato water for a yummy salad dressing or use with pasta.

> Tony's Tip!
>
> This tomato blend can be tossed with leafy greens such as arugula, spinach or other greens. This can also be used with pasta or rice.

Satiating Snacks, Blissful Beverages & Delectable Desserts

That's right; there are meals between meals... in the nutrition world, we call them snacks! These satiating snacks play a big role in weight loss. By eating healthy snacks between meals, it helps keep portions in check for main meals. The other benefit of healthy snacking is it stabilizes blood glucose levels and curbs cravings for refined foods as the day progresses. The best defense is a good offense. My main go-to snack and the savior for those in the MODA Nation support group is the MODA Snack Pack.

I encourage you to eat your fruits and vegetables any chance you get. Occasionally I would have a blend of fruits and vegetables as an evening treat or in a pinch as a meal replacement. And yes, you even get dessert!

Carb-Based Snacks

- Grain crackers such as 2–3 Finn Crisp + fruit or vegetables
- 1 cup popped popcorn, flavored with cinnamon, pumpkin spice, cayenne pepper or dehydrated fruit
- Quinoa + hemp
- Quinoa + cranberries
- Quinoa + hint of Parmesan cheese
- Quinoa + vegetables
- ½ cup quinoa + ¾ cup plain yogurt
- Plain yogurt with fruit (frozen fruit makes for "ice cream" effect) = 1 dairy serving + fruit serving

Protein-Based Snacks

- 1 mini can tuna
- 1 hardboiled egg
- 1 tablespoon peanut butter + celery
- 1 tablespoon peanut butter + apple wedges
- ½ cup peeled edamame
- 2–3 tablespoons hemp shot
- ¾ cup unflavored Greek yogurt
- ¾ cup unflavored Greek yogurt + fruit
- ½ cup cottage cheese + fruit

> ### Tony's Tip!
>
> Nut butter should only have one ingredient: the nut!

Protein + Carb Snack Ideas:

Healthy Elvis: Peanut butter + banana + hemp (optional) on grain bread or grain crackers
2–3 tablespoons hummus on 2 grain crackers

MODA Snack Pack

Makes one Snack Pack
Ingredients:
½ ounce shredded wheat
1–2 Finn Crisp, broken into pieces
10 almonds
5 halves walnuts
3 Brazil nuts
¼ cup of dehydrated fruit, raisins, Turkish apricots, Goji berries

Directions:
Combine all ingredients in Tupperware container. Make several for the week as part of Snack Prep.

Lite Elvis on Hemp Hors-d'oeuvres

Ingredients:
Finn Crisp, Wasa Bread or Fazer Crisp crackers
1 banana, sliced
Natural peanut or nut butter
Hemp seeds (hearts)
Cinnamon

Directions:
Break crackers in half.
Spread very light layer of peanut butter on cracker.
Sprinkle hemp on peanut butter.
Top with sliced banana. Dust with cinnamon.

Tony's Tip!

Fresh grated nutmeg on yogurt makes for a sweet, savory treat.

Ginger Tea

Serves 2
Ingredients:
2 cups water
½ cup thickly sliced ginger
Juice of 1 lemon

Directions:
Combine water and ginger pieces in a saucepan.
Bring to a boil and simmer for 3–5 minutes on low heat. Remove from heat.
Scoop out ginger pieces.
Pour liquid into a mug and add lemon juice.

Green Iced Tea

Serves 4
Ingredients:
4 cups boiling water
4–5 green tea bags
1–2 tablespoons honey (optional)
Lemon

Directions:
Place boiling water into heatproof pitcher with tea bags. Steep for
5–10 minutes.
Remove tea bags and add honey (if using).
Allow to sit or chill.
Pour into ice-filled glass.
Squeeze fresh lemon juice.

> Tony's Tip!
>
> Consuming a sufficient amount of water is key to weight loss success. These teas make great refreshing alternatives.

Cocoa Banana Milkshake

Serves 1
Ingredients:
1 medium ripe banana
1 cup milk, soy or almond milk
½ cup ice
1 tablespoon cocoa power

Directions:
Place ingredients into blender then blitz until smooth.

Yogurt Banana Smoothie

Serves 1–2
Ingredients:
1 ripe medium banana
½–1 cup ice
½ cup milk, soy or almond milk
½ cup whole or instant oats
4 heaping tablespoons unflavored Greek yogurt
2 heaping tablespoons whey protein
1 tablespoon ground flax seed
1 teaspoon vanilla extract

Directions:
Place ingredients into blender then blitz until smooth.

Fruit & Ginger Smoothie

Serves 1–2
Ingredients:
½–1 cup ice
½ cup milk, soy or almond milk
½ cup fruit such as banana, apple, pear or chopped pineapple
4 heaping tablespoon unflavored Greek yogurt
2 heaping tablespoons whey protein
Fresh ginger, grated (as much as desired)

Directions:
Place ingredients into blender then blitz until smooth.

Peach Bliss Smoothies

Serves 1
Ingredients:
1 cup frozen peaches
¾ cup milk, soy or almond milk
½ teaspoon pure vanilla extract

Directions:
Place ingredients into blender then blitz until smooth.

> **Tony's Tip!**
>
> Always be sure to give peaches a good wash.

Oatmeal, Flax & Fruit Smoothie

Serves 1–2
Ingredients:
1 ripe medium banana
1 cup milk, soy or almond milk
½–1 cup ice
½ cup whole or instant oats
3 tablespoons ground flax seed

Directions:
Place ingredients into blender then blitz until smooth.

> **Tony's Tip!**
>
> Substitute any fruit for banana in this smoothie.

Coconut Quinoa Pudding

Serves 4
Ingredients:
½ cup quinoa
½ cup water
1 teaspoon cinnamon
¼ teaspoon ground cloves or ground allspice
½ cup milk, almond or coconut milk
1 teaspoon pure vanilla extract
½ cup of favorite fruit (berries are great for this) or unsweetened dried cranberries or raisins
½ cup shredded unsweetened coconut
Fresh nutmeg (optional)

Directions:
Rinse quinoa well under cold water using fine mesh strainer.
Combine quinoa, water, milk, vanilla, cinnamon and cloves in heavy saucepan.
Cook covered on medium high until mixture comes to a slow boil. Cover and boil for 10 minutes. Let simmer on lowest heat with the lid off for 4–5 minutes, stirring occasionally.
Add fruit and coconut. Stir and let simmer with the lid off for another 4–5 minutes. Turn off heat, cover and let sit until ready to serve.
Serve warm or cold and dust with fresh nutmeg.

Lemon Ricotta Pudding

Serves 4
Ingredients:
2 lemons
2 cups ricotta cheese
Fresh nutmeg, as much as desired

Directions:
Remove rind from lemons and set aside.
Combine ricotta cheese and squeeze in lemon juice. Cover and allow to sit for 1–4 hours in refrigerator. Spoon mixture into ring molds or bowls.
Garnish with lemon rind and grate with fresh nutmeg.

Berry Parfait

Serves 2
Ingredients:
1 cup unflavored Greek yogurt
½ cup berries of choice
Fresh nutmeg, as much as desired

Directions:
Mix fruit and yogurt in medium bowl.
Spoon into Tupperware containers.
Grate fresh nutmeg on top.

> **Tony's Tip!**
>
> Ricotta can be substitued in place of cottage cheese or vice versa.

Orange Pumpkin Parfait

Serves 2
Ingredients:
1 orange
6 ounces soft tofu or 1 cup unflavored Greek yogurt
1 (16 ounce) can pure pumpkin purée

Directions:
Preheat oven 375°F. Remove orange rind and place on tinfoil-lined baking dish.
Bake rind for 10–12 minutes. Remove from oven and set aside.
In a medium bowl, break tofu into small pieces. Add peaches and squeeze in orange juice. Mash fruit for a smooth consistency or whisk fruit pieces into yogurt.
Spoon mixture into a visually appealing bowl or martini glass.
Garnish with cooked orange rind.
Variant: Substitute lemon in place of orange.

Delectable Desserts

Cool Cucumber Blended Parfait

Serves 1
Ingredients:
1 medium apple or pear, cored
1 cup cucumber, cut into chunks
½ cup plain yogurt
Ice

Directions:
Place ingredients into blender and blitz until smooth.

Banana Parfait Martini

Serves 2
Ingredients:
1 large banana (the riper the better)
1 cup unflavored Greek yogurt
Fresh nutmeg, as much as desired

Directions:
Mash banana in bowl using a fork.
Stir in yogurt.
Spoon into martini glass.
Grate fresh nutmeg on top.
Top with fruit if desired.

Tony's Tip!

This makes a great evening dessert or snack. Plus it's a great healthy dessert for kids or place in small Tupperware containers for a snack on the go and pack in lunch box.

Killer Kale Blended Parfait

Serves 1
Ingredients:
1 medium apple or pear, cored
1 cup chopped or frozen kale
½ cup plain yogurt
1–2 tablespoon honey
Ice

Directions:
Place ingredients into blender and blitz until smooth.

Tony's Tip!

Substitute fresh sliced peaches.

Mini Berry Parfait in a Mug

Serves 2
Ingredients:
¾ cup unflavored Greek yogurt
1 cup sliced fresh strawberries
½ cup fresh blueberries

Directions:
Place yogurt in bottom of bowl or small coffee mug.
Decoratively top with fresh fruit.

The Ultimate Fruit Salad

Serves 4
Ingredients:
2 cups fresh strawberries, washed, hulled and sliced
2 cups fresh blueberries, washed
1 mango, chopped into chunks
Juice of 2 limes

Directions:
Combine fruit in sealable container.
Stir in lime juice.
Allow to sit for 1–12 hours.
Spoon into visually appealing bowl or martini glass.

Tony's Tip!

The acid in the lime will extract much of the natural sugars in the fruit and create a delectable glaze.

Final Tidbits

Getting started can be the most challenging part of this journey – it was for me. Many, myself included, look too far ahead; instead focus on one day at a time.

"The journey of a thousand miles begins with one step." — Lao Tzu

- Be sure to have goals. I encourage you to have short and long term goals. I suggest that your first long term goal be to lose five percent of your body weight. Once you get over that hump, empowered by that success, you will build momentum to carry you to your healthy body weight.
- Remind yourself constantly why you decided to take on this journey: a motive is what induces a person to act, keeping you focused on your goal. Make you your priority.
- This journey is not a straight downward line. Understand that you will likely have bad days and mishaps along the way. Make every effort to avoid them, but when they happen, accept it and move on. Do not dwell on any mishap.
- Surrender. As Eckhart Tolle says, "Surrender is the simple but profound wisdom of yielding to rather than opposing the flow of life." Or as my good friend Roy says, "Stop fighting it!"

Fasten your seatbelt for the most rewarding ride of your life – an incredible journey to happy, healthy, long, MODAlicious living.

Avoid Getting Swindled at the Supermarket

It's a no-brainer; the supermarket is not what it used to be. It is now a vast landscape of sugar-covered confections, salty snacks and fatty gratifications. But it's not only the supermarket that has temptations at checkout: Retail outlets, drugstores and even hardware stores now force you through a maze of processed foods, all calling your name, whispering *"buy me."* Many of these items are at your children's eye level. Coincidence? Not a chance.

With the advent of modern graphic design, manufacturers and distributors use creative food packaging and displays that can trigger the pleasure center in the brain, causing the consumer to crave it and ultimately buy it. Use the following list as a start to the supermarket:

- Never shop hungry! If this is not possible, eat a healthy snack, salad or some fruit first.
- Avoid shopping late in the day when you are tired.
- Have an idea of what items you have in your kitchen and what you really need. Create a list.
- Most healthy food items will be found on the perimeter of the grocery store. Departments such as produce, bakery, meat, seafood and dairy are along the edge of the store. Very few healthy items will be in the centre aisles, though some exceptions exist.
- Avoid relying on claims made on the front of packaging. Be sure to read the ingredient list on packaged foods. Be the gatekeeper. Take charge of healthy purchasing decisions. If you don't put it into your cart, it won't enter your home and eventually go into your mouth. Remember my mantra: "Your home must be in the zone!"
- Distract yourself at checkout. This is where most impulse decisions are made.

Produce

- Eat a rainbow. Choose a variety of colors when buying fruits and vegetables. Each different color offers specific phytochemicals, flavoineds and antioxidants
- Experiment and try new fruits and vegetables to keep meals exciting
- Buy vegetables that you can eat as snacks like baby carrots, peppers, cucumbers, cherry tomatoes, etc.
- Purchase leafy greens or pre-washed greens to have ready-to-eat salads
- Plant-based proteins such as soy, tofu or tempeh are found in the refrigerated produce section

Bread and Baked Goods

- When choosing breads, be sure to choose 100% whole wheat whole grain such as Ezekiel
- As for baked goods: Just stay away!

Final Tidbits

The Middle Aisles

The items below are items you will need to dart into the middle aisles for.

- Canned fish (salmon, tuna, sardines, etc.)
- Legumes and lentils
- Cereals
- Plain mustard
- Vinegars
- Hot Sauce
- Whole grain crackers
- Canned and frozen vegetables and fruits
- Rice and whole grain pasta
- Stock
- Beverages: water, tea and coffee
- Nuts, seeds and natural nut butters
- Dried fruit

Poultry & Fish

- Select white meats (chicken and turkey)
- When purchasing ground chicken or turkey, go for extra-lean rather than lean whenever possible
- Select only leaner cuts of pork or beef (round or loin)
- Choose leaner deli meats such as chicken or turkey. Roasted cuts tend to be lower in sodium than smoked

Dairy

- Choose 1–2% milk
- Choose plain, unflavored varieties of 2% yogurt. Most fruit yogurts have added sugar. Purchase plain yogurt and add your own fruit
- Select artisanal cheese. Avoid processed cheese
- Choose free-range omega eggs. Price definitely matters when it comes to quality of eggs

Useful Staples to Keep on Hand

Refrigerator

- 1–2% milk or fortified dairy beverage, such as soy or almond milk
- 2% cottage cheese
- 2% plain yogurt
- 2% Greek yogurt
- Protein such as chicken, fish and alternatives
- Variety of fruit
- Wide selection of vegetables

Freezer

- Proteins (chicken and fish)
- Frozen vegetables
- Frozen fruit
- Leftover prepared meals
- Frozen Ezekiel bread

Pantry

- Mustard
- Vinegars: balsamic, red or white wine, apple cider, rice wine, etc.
- Hot sauce
- Spices: black pepper, paprika, oregano, Mrs. Dash, etc.
- Jarred peppers: roasted and hot
- Strained tomatoes
- Whole canned tomatoes
- Horseradish
- Jarred garlic, pre-minced
- Olive oil in dark glass or tin container
- Sesame oil
- Cooking spray
- Nuts and seeds
- Hemp/chia/flax seeds
- Canned tuna, salmon and sardines
- Legumes, dried or canned (select low-sodium)
- Lentils, dried or canned
- Low-sodium chicken or vegetable stock
- Whole wheat flatbreads such as pita or naan
- Whole grain crackers: Finn Crisp, Ryvita, Wasa Bread, matzo, etc.
- Shredded wheat or Muffets cereal
- Cooked cereals such as Red River or Bob's Red Mill
- Whole and steel-cut oats
- 100% whole wheat bread
- Sourdough bread
- Porridge
- Barley
- Bulgur
- Millet/amaranth
- Quinoa
- Whole wheat pasta
- Couscous
- Rice: brown, red, wild, etc.
- Wheat bran/germ
- Psyllium husk
- Dried vegetable such as tomatoes or mushrooms
- Dehydrated fruit: Raisins or Turkish apricots, etc.
- Tea
- Bottled water

> **Tony's Tip!**
>
> Make mustard the condiment of choice. It's tasty, nutritious and practically calorie free. Steer clear of sweet mustards.

My Checklist towards Success:

- Manage hunger by eating regularly
- Have breakfast within 90 minutes of waking
- Eat a grain carbohydrate (preferably cooked cereal) at breakfast (avoid bread at breakfast and dinner)
- Eat lean- or plant-based protein at every meal
- Eat lots of vegetables (6–12 servings a day)
- Have lunch 4–5 hours after breakfast
- Have dinner 5–6 hours after lunch
- Drink sufficient water
- Avoid fruit juice, soda and diet soda
- Plan meals once or twice a week
- Accurately record your food and drink intake daily
- Use a food scale to weigh or measure quantities
- Don't skip meals
- Eat slowly and mindfully
- Beware of hunger imposters: fatigue, thirst, boredom, anxiety, sadness, frustration, etc.
- Reward yourself with non-food items
- Stay active
- Hold yourself accountable for your weight loss
- Get sufficient restful sleep (7–8 hours)
- Monitor any medications
- Continue to set goals
- Continue to reaffirm why you are on this journey
- Surround yourself with like-minded people
- Review this list frequently

So Many to Thank

This journey, MODA and this book would not have been possible without the help, inspiration, support and efforts of many.

First to my parents, Tanya and Joe. Both have been incredibly supportive during my weight loss and maintenance. My endless love and gratitude for their tremendous support and encouragement as I pursue my nutrition mission.

To Nevenka and Zuzana. Both understood the challenges at various stages of my weight loss and maintenance and help keep me "clean." Thank you.

To Helen K. No journey is ever a straight line. Thank you so much for your words of encouragement, sisterly advice, and mostly importantly for being such good-hearted person.

Team 2Socail, Lauren and Steve, both of whom made a world of difference in providing MODA its social exposure and professional MODA image.

To Michael, Jim, Tarick, Peter, Scott and John who helped guide this confused soul in launching MODA and helped it to come to fruition.

This book could not have been possible without the efforts of Jordi Hayman, Rachel Little, Colleen and Rob.

To Rob Laman. I owe you a great deal of gratitude for all the time and effort providing guidance during the development of this book. You always found the time. Thank you so much. I'm truly grateful our paths have crossed once again after several years.

To friends Dale, Greg, Peter, Yoemil and Mark for being so supportive throughout my journey, understanding that certain places were off limits and being accommodating in places to eat.

To all my instructors at George Brown and University of Toronto. To Dr. Vera Tarman, you have become a much-needed mentor and coach to me. Even before meeting you, your book *Food Junkies* was a huge inspiration during my journey.

Anthony Di Pasquale, you taught me a ton on nutrition. Thanks bro! You rule!

To my family doctor, Dr. T. You helped nudge me with your advice. I'm grateful for your patience in a time I did not "get it."

To all the folks that became part of MODA Nation in the early days. A big MODA thanks for the confidence and support to get MODA off the ground.

There have been many that encouraged me to continue to pursue my dreams and follow through on my mission be a Man On A Nutrition Mission™. To each and everyone one of you: Thank you!

To Jason and Mary, who have given me the opportunity of a lifetime to produce the documentary *Follow Me*. To Nicholas Li, videographer extraordinaire. It's been a blast to work with you.

Last and certainly not least, to you, the reader. I thought losing my weight would be one of the most gratifying things of my life but as it turns out the ability to give back and educate others has turned out to be even more gratifying.

I encourage you to reach out to me with any questions or comments you have. Tony@ModaNutrition.com
http://modanutrition.com/testimonials/

Made in United States
North Haven, CT
24 October 2021